In the event of death...

Wills and Inheritance in Scotland

DAVID IAN NICHOLS, M.A., Ph.D.
Writer to the Signet

Published by Scottish Legal Education Trust
ISBN 0 9507056 0 8
and Scottish Association of Citizens Advice Bureaux
ISBN 0 905831 02 0

Printed by   Lindsay & Co. Ltd., Edinburgh

Guide to Contents

B

Preface

This book is a layman's guide to the Scottish law of death, wills and inheritance. It concentrates on the wills and estates of Scottish people, and makes no attempt to deal with foreigners who leave property in Scotland. There are considerable differences between Scotland and England in these areas, both in the law and in the procedures that have to be followed, so that books dealing with English law will mislead any Scottish reader.

In contrast to England, Scotland has few up-to-date legal text books. Gloag and Henderson, *Introduction to the Law of Scotland* (8th ed.) due to be published soon by W. Green & Son Ltd., and Walker, *Principles of Scottish Private Law* (2nd ed.) published in 1975 by Clarendon Press, Oxford, contain sections on wills and inheritance of property, while the law of intestate succession is treated in detail in Meston, *The Succession (Scotland) Act 1964* (2nd ed.) published in 1969 by W. Green & Son Ltd. These books should be consulted by anybody who is interested in studying further.

I wish to thank the Scottish Legal Education Trust and the Scottish Association of Citizens Advice Bureaux for making this publication possible, and Mrs Frances Allen, Professor Eric Clive, Mr Alastair Brownlie, Mr Ken Swinton and my wife, Dr Janet Alison for their many helpful comments and encouragement. I also wish to thank Miss Jean Robertson for typing the manuscript.

The law is hopefully correct up to 1 June 1980. The costs mentioned in the text can, in these inflationary days, only be regarded as a guide to current amounts.

David Nichols
June 1980

CHAPTER 1.

Practical Arrangements after a Death

This chapter is directed at the family of the deceased and tells them what has to be done immediately after death: the doctor's certificate; registration of the death; arrangements for the burial or cremation; dealing with any bequest of parts of the deceased's body; and finding the will.

Death certificate

When a person dies the death must be certified by a doctor. The doctor who has been attending the deceased will normally issue a certificate of death without any difficulty. If the doctor has not been attending the deceased person recently (e.g. death may have occurred very suddenly) or if there were unusual circumstances, he may not feel able to issue a certificate. Where the death is sudden, accidental or suspicious the local procurator fiscal is informed. The doctor will advise the relatives about this. The procurator fiscal may obtain statements from witnesses or others who have useful information or he may order a post mortem examination of the body to be carried out. If the death was accidental but the circumstances require further investigation a fatal accident inquiry will be held. This is obligatory when death takes place at work. If it seems as if the death was caused by criminal or negligent actions the procurator fiscal and the police will carry on the investigation to discover which person or persons may be responsible.

Registration of death

The death must be registered within eight days with the Registrar of Births, Deaths and Marriages. Normally registration is made at the local office for the area in which the death took place or for the area in which the deceased person lived. Special provisions apply for the notification and registration of deaths which have occurred aboard ships or in aircraft.

The death may be registered not only by any relative of the deceased, but also by any person present at the death, the deceased's executor (see page 6) or other legal representative, the occupier of premises where the death took place or any other person possessing the information needed for registration. Failure to register a death will result in reminders being sent to those liable and eventually legal proceedings may be taken to obtain the necessary information.

C

The Registrar needs to see the medical certificate of death or to be given the name and address of a doctor who can be asked to give the certificate. The deceased person's birth and marriage (if appropriate) certificates should also be taken along together with his National Health Service medical card and any state pension or benefit books if these can be found. The Registrar will enter personal details of the deceased and the date and place of death in the register and ask the informant to check it carefully and sign the entry.

A certificate of registration of the death will be issued free of charge. This is needed by the undertaker before he can carry out the funeral. The Registrar will also issue, where applicable, special free certificates for National Insurance purposes (e.g. death grant). A larger document called an extract death certificate can also be obtained. This is a copy of the entry made in the register of deaths and is needed to prove the death, in order, for example, to claim money under life insurance policies. Other organisations may require to see an extract death certificate as well. The current cost is £1.50 for each extract certificate issued when the death is registered. If a certificate is ordered after the death has been registered extra search fees will be charged.

Burial or Cremation

Arrangements for the funeral are made through an undertaker or funeral director. He will arrange for the body to be removed and will, if asked, see to death notices in the papers and contact a minister to officiate at the service. The alternative methods for disposal of bodies are burial and cremation. Burial is always allowed. If the deceased person had ground in a cemetery, the burial ground or lair certificate should be handed to the undertaker.

Cremation is only allowed if the deceased person did not forbid it. It is important therefore to look at the will (if there is one) to check that it does not contain a prohibition of cremation or state a preference for burial. A relative or the executor has to apply to the Medical Referee of the Cremation Authority for permission to cremate. The undertaker will help with the application forms. The applicant must state that to the best of his knowledge the deceased did not forbid cremation. The executor (see page 6) or next-of-kin can override the deceased's desire to be cremated and if there is any family dispute permission to cremate will almost certainly be refused. The family can in practice ignore the deceased's desire to be cremated, should they wish to do so, by not applying for permission for the body to be cremated. The doctor who signed the medical death certificate must certify that he is satisfied as to the cause of death and the body should then be examined by a second doctor who must also be satisfied. If the procurator fiscal has been involved then his consent to cremation must be obtained as well. If the death was in any way suspicious cremation may be refused. Once the body is burned there is no way of conducting a post mortem examination for traces of poison etc. whereas a buried body can be exhumed.

Bequest of body to hospital

Many people express a wish to bequeath their bodies to a hospital for medical research. The Anatomy Acts 1832 to 1871 were passed to allow bodies to be provided for anatomy schools or medical research in a regular and above board manner rather than by the activities of "resurrectionists" and people like Burke and Hare. If the deceased refused permission then his body cannot be disposed of in this way. Even if the deceased wished his body to be used for medical research the surviving spouse or other relatives have a veto. When death occurs, the hospital may not be in a position to take up the offer and the body will have to be buried or cremated in the normal manner. If the body is accepted the hospital can keep it for up to two years. Any funeral service should be carried out before acceptance, since after the hospital has finished with the body, they normally bury or cremate it without notifying the family.

The Human Tissue Act 1961 allows parts of a body to be used in surgery. Kidneys can be transplanted to suitable patients, saving their lives, while eyes can be used after death to restore somebody else's sight. Parts can only be taken if the deceased wished it and again relatives have a right of veto. If kidneys are to be of any use they must be removed very soon after death and the normal methods of obtaining permission from next-of-kin are usually too slow. Kidney donor cards, which many people carry with them indicate that they wish their kidneys to be used and that the next-of-kin do not object. Even so before removal the hospital try to contact the family to make sure there is still no objection before removing the kidneys. After any organs have been removed, the body is returned to the family for burial or cremation.

Arrangements for the funeral

A relative or friend usually contacts the undertaker and makes arrangements for the funeral. Where the death takes place in a hospital or nursing home and nobody else assumes responsibility for the funeral arrangements, the hospital or home either asks the regional council's social work department to take over or they make the arrangements themselves. If no one else arranges the funeral the district council has a duty to bury or cremate anyone who dies in its area.

Liability to pay for the funeral

The person or organisation ordering the funeral is liable to pay the undertaker. The cost can be recovered out of any property (including an insurance policy) left by the deceased, and reasonable funeral expenses take priority over any other debts or claims on the deceased's property. Where not enough money is left, the surviving spouse or the parents of a child under 16 are liable to pay, if the funeral was carried out by the local authority. Apart from these cases, a relative who has not ordered the funeral is not legally liable for the cost.

Help with funeral costs

Even a modest funeral will today cost upwards of £200 by the time all the burial or cremation fees are included. Many undertakers will carry out a very simple funeral at a specially low price.

To help with funeral expenses a National Insurance death grant (currently up to a maximum of £30) may be claimed. No grant is payable on the death of a man born before 5 July 1883 or a woman born before 5 July 1888. A reduced grant is payable on the death of a child below 16. There is no means test for the grant as it is a benefit paid out of National Insurance contributions. The person paying for the funeral applies for a grant to a local office of the Department of Health and Social Security. The free death certificate issued by the Registrar of Births, Deaths and Marriages needs to be sent with the application.

Apart from this death grant a person on supplementary benefit can apply to the Department of Health and Social Security for an exceptional needs payment to cover the cost of a close relative's funeral, if the deceased left no money and there is no one else in the family who can afford to pay. The Department should be contacted before arrangements for the funeral are made since they will not pay for any expenses that have already been incurred.

The regional council's social work department may also be able to help with funeral expenses. They are only likely to do so, however, if the deceased was in their care or had been receiving assistance from them. Many trade unions or friendly societies will pay for the funerals of their members.

Finding the will

As soon as a person dies a search should be made for his or her will. This should be done before the funeral arrangements are made as the will may contain specific instructions about this or contain a prohibition against cremation.

The first place to look for a will is among the deceased's documents either at home or at the bank. Even if no will can be found there might be a copy or letters indicating where the will might be. When a lawyer makes a will for a client he usually keeps the original in a safe in his office and gives the client a copy. If nothing is found the deceased's lawyer should be contacted to see if he has a will. A home-made will may present more difficulties for it can be tucked away in an unexpected place and the family might be unaware that a will was ever made. If no will can be found, but a will is thought to exist, advertisements can be placed in newspapers and legal periodicals asking for any lawyer, banker or other person who has a will to let the family know.

Any will found may not be the most recent one. A later will might well exist particularly where the one found is very old or where the deceased had married or been divorced after making it.

PRACTICAL ARRANGEMENTS AFTER A DEATH

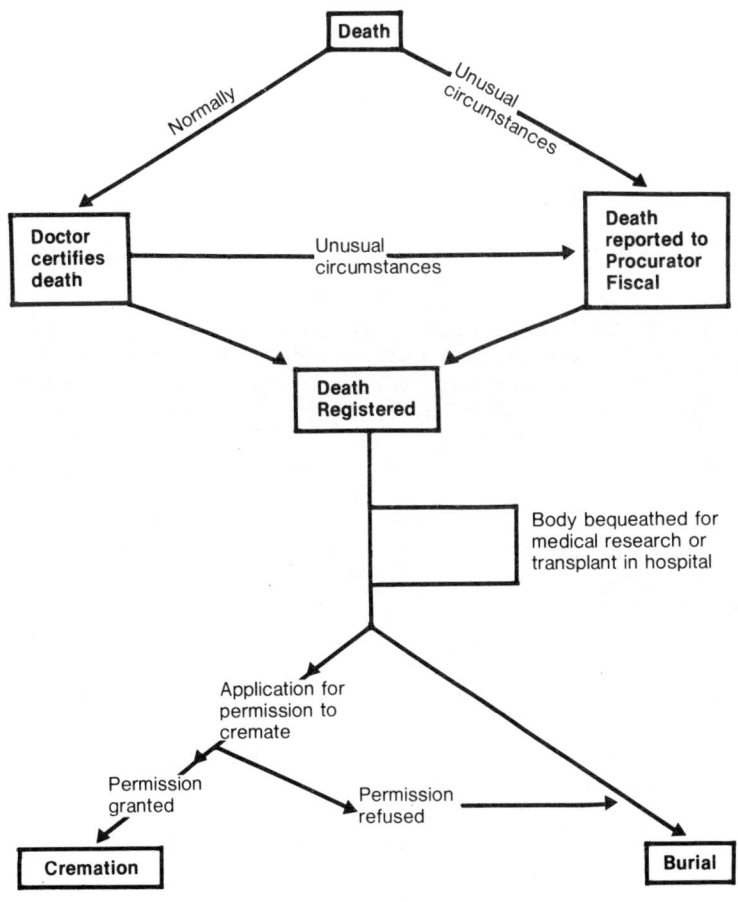

CHAPTER 2

The Initial Steps in Dealing with an Estate

This chapter is directed at the family of the deceased and more particularly to the particular friends or relatives who have been appointed as executors by the deceased to deal with his property after his death. It also describes how executors are appointed when the deceased leaves no instructions. As well as describing how executors are approved or confirmed, the chapter discusses how the executors should set about making an inventory of the estate and how they should collect in the various items before distribution to beneficiaries goes ahead.

EXECUTORS

Executors are people who pay the deceased's debts, any taxes and expenses and distribute his property to those entitled to it. They are either appointed by the deceased in his will or appointed by the court. If there is a will it usually names the executor(s) the deceased wished to deal with or administer his estate. Sometimes no executor is named in the will or the person(s) may have died already or refuse to act. In these cases the court will appoint the person who inherits the whole property or the residue of the estate (see page 50) as executor. Being an executor often involves a lot of work but the executor will not be paid unless the will provides for this. A person who is old or ill may not wish to become involved, and should then sign a statement saying that he declines to accept being an executor. If only one executor is named, he should not decline since this involves the extra expense and delay of an application to the court for someone else to be appointed. Rather he should appoint another person to act as executor with him and then resign himself. The appointed executor can then act alone.

An executor may decide to decline if he lives abroad. It is often necessary for quick decisions to be made about the disposal of property (e.g. whether to accept an offer for the house) and this can be very difficult to arrange if one of the executors is in, say, Australia. Even if this situation does not arise considerable delays are caused by having to post abroad every document requiring the executor's signature. If there are other executors in Britain then the executor abroad might be asked tactfully if he really wishes to become involved in the day-to-day administration or whether he would be content to let the other executors act but to be kept informed of the progress made. Another way of dealing with this problem is for the executor abroad to empower a person in Scotland (usually the solicitor dealing with the estate) to act for him.

When no will is left the court will appoint an executor (called an executor dative) to administer the property. The surviving spouse who takes the whole estate by virtue of prior rights (see page 23) is entitled to be appointed the sole executor. Even if some other members of the family are entitled to share in the estate, the surviving spouse is usually made an executor, although the others can apply to be appointed as well. The surviving spouse may feel unable to take on the task of being an executor. In this case one of the children can be appointed whether or not they have any share in the deceased's estate.

The intending executor applies to the sheriff court of the area in which the deceased was domiciled (see glossary) by petition asking to be appointed executor dative (see glossary). A different procedure is followed for small estates (see page 16). The petition is displayed on the notice board in the sheriff court for a few days and is then granted if no objection has been received. A petition will cost at least £30 in legal fees and court dues, more than the cost of a simple will appointing executors.

An executor who misbehaves or fails to carry out his duties can be removed by the court and others may be added if some of those who benefit feel their interests are not being looked after properly. These are all extreme measures and should only be used when absolutely necessary and when more informal methods have been tried without success.

Do you need a solicitor?

Executors may deal with and distribute the deceased person's property by themselves. However, for any but the simplest estate being an executor involves a lot of time and effort. The legal forms and proceedings may be confusing and a mistake in interpreting the will or forgetting to pay some debt or tax may result in the executor having to meet claims out of his own pocket. These burdens are heavy especially where the executor is a close relative of the deceased person.

Executors should seriously consider asking a solicitor to deal with the estate for them. This is one of the main types of work a general family solicitor does and he should have considerable expertise in this area. Where the estate is a small estate (see page 16) the sheriff clerk will do some of the legal work for the executor. For larger estates executors who wish to proceed without legal assistance have to prepare all the necessary documents themselves. Even for small estates, the work the sheriff clerk does is only a small part of the total work involved, and most executors feel the need for the assistance and guidance a lawyer can provide.

Normally the deceased's solicitor is chosen by the executors. This has advantages in that he is familiar with his late client's affairs and need not spend a lot of time on preliminary investigations. Otherwise an executor can ask his own solicitor to assist him.

Legal costs

The fees a lawyer charges depend mainly on the total value of the estate and how much work is involved. His fees are an expense of dealing with the estate and are payable out of it. The current scale of charges permitted by the Law Society of Scotland can be obtained from them, any solicitor or a Citizens Advice Bureau. At present the fee for an estate valued at £5,000 would be £240, and for an estate valued at £25,000, nearly £1,000. Unless the work has been unduly heavy these are the maximum fees that can be charged. Most lawyers will charge less than the maximum, particularly for small estates, or where the estate consists of a house and a few other items. The executor and members of the family can help keep down charges by doing some of the work themselves. They could list the deceased's property themselves, advertise and show the house, dispose of the car and furniture and leave the solicitor with only the strictly legal work to do.

An executor who feels he has been overcharged should raise the matter with the solicitor first. If no agreement is reached the executor can ask the solicitor to have his account checked or "taxed" by an independent official known as an auditor. If he does so he should bear in mind that he will have to pay for this taxing, together with as much of the original bill as the auditor considers reasonable.

Publishing the will

It is not the custom in Scotland to have a formal reading of the will to the family after the funeral, but people are told as soon as convenient what has been left to them. The solicitor will normally attend to this but executors may prefer to tell close relatives themselves. Copies of the will are normally sent to the widow(er) and children and to any person who has been left a legacy of the residue (see page 50) of the estate. Others who have been left a sum of money or some specific item (e.g. a piece of jewellery) need only be sent letters informing them of their legacies.

It is a good idea to register a will as soon as possible in case it gets lost. The loss of a will can have extremely serious consequences. A draft or a copy can be declared by the Court of Session to be equivalent to the lost will but this process costs upwards of £300. If no drafts or copies remain the deceased's property may have to be disposed of as if he had never made a will.

A will can, for a small fee, be registered either in the local sheriff court register or in the national register called the Books of Council and Session (or the Register of Deeds) kept at Edinburgh. When a will is registered it is retained for safe keeping, and an official copy called an extract issued. If an extract gets lost another can always be obtained which is just as valid as the first one.

Once a will has been registered it becomes a public document. Anyone, on payment of a small fee, is entitled to see it and obtain a copy. Some registers go back many centuries and this makes them useful in investigating family histories.

LISTING THE ESTATE

The executor's first major task is to prepare, with the help of the lawyer, a list of all the property (e.g. money, furniture, investments or house) the deceased owned or had an interest in. This is called inventorying the estate. The list must be complete and the executor will have to swear that this is so to the best of his knowledge and belief. It is a serious criminal offence to conceal property to avoid paying tax or to hide it from beneficiaries. In addition to all the property in Scotland, items in other parts of the United Kingdom and abroad must also be included. Sometimes items are missed out, perhaps because they were not discovered in time. When this happens a separate list of the omitted items must be made up and an additional confirmation called an eik (pronounced "eek") obtained. This is extra trouble and expense, so that it is well worth while carrying out the initial investigations as thoroughly as possible.

Each item must also be valued on the basis of what it would have fetched on the open market at the *date of death*. This is necessary because capital transfer tax is (or may be) payable on the total value of the property (see page 15). Some items such as money in a bank account or shares can be valued accurately, but for furniture, a house or perhaps even a car the value is much more a matter of opinion. For these last items the executor, aided by the solicitor or an expert valuator, should estimate the value as well as he can. The value put in at this stage is only provisional and can be changed later if, for example, the property is sold at a different price later on. If the Capital Taxes Office think the value of any item has been set too low they will query it. If it is too high they are unlikely to challenge it so it is better to err on the low side.

The following paragraphs go through some of the more usual items and Appendix II contains a specimen inventory.

House

If the house is owned the executor will have to find out what the deceased's rights in it were. He may have owned all of it, or only a share of it, but the position may be more complex. Unless the executor knows what the position is, the titles to the house should be examined by a lawyer.

A house rented from a local authority or housing association should not be put in the inventory. This is because it has no value to the tenant as he cannot sell his right to live in it. The same is normally true where the property is rented from a private landlord, but sometimes (e.g. a croft or a farm) the tenant can sell his right of tenancy and then the property must be included in the inventory. The widow(er) or children may be entitled to take over a private tenancy. The Tenants' Rights, Etc. (Scotland) Bill, currently being discussed in Parliament, will extend this entitlement to local authority or housing association tenancies.

The valuation of a house is not easy. If it is going to be sold then only a rough value need be put down at this stage, since the precise value will be known later from the highest offer. If it is not going to be sold a good estimate can be obtained from what similar houses have fetched recently, or it might be worth getting a survey and valuation in case a dispute with the Capital Taxes Office develops later on. A half share of a house is now treated as worth exactly one-half of the value of the whole property. If the deceased had only a liferent (i.e. he could stay in the house during his life but on his death it passed to someone else) the value for his estate is calculated as if he had owned it absolutely. For other situations expert advice is needed from a lawyer and perhaps a surveyor as well.

Bank, Savings Bank and Building Society Accounts

Passbooks, cheque books and statements should be looked for amongst the deceased's papers. Each organisation should be written to, telling them of the death and asking for a note of the balance (plus interest if any) due at the date of death. They should also be asked whether they have any other accounts in the name of the deceased either solely or jointly. Banks may have property or documents in safe custody or as security for loans made to the deceased.

If the account was in the name of the deceased only, then the whole balance is treated as belonging to him. With a joint account the amount regarded as belonging to the deceased depends on whether or not the other joint account holder put in any money. If only the deceased put money in (e.g. a joint account in name of husband and wife with only the husband's salary going in) then the whole balance is still treated as belonging to the deceased. If the other person contributed as well (e.g. husband and wife both earning) then only half the balance is regarded as belonging to the deceased.

After a bank has been notified of the death, the deceased's account is frozen and no further payments can be made, except to the executors after they have been confirmed. A joint account can however still be used by the survivor. This can be a very useful source of cash for a widow(er) immediately after the death before pensions or other payments come in.

Furniture and personal possessions

Only articles belonging to the deceased should be included. Strictly, hire-purchase goods should be valued and the amount still due on them deducted with only the balance being put in the inventory. Unless the hire-purchase goods are particularly valuable, for example a car, it is normal not to include them at all. It is impossible to list every item of furniture, or personal possessions separately. An entry such as "Furniture, plenishings and personal effects belonging to the deceased valued at . . ." is quite sufficient. Each major item should, however, be roughly valued in order to arrive at a fair figure for the total. Unless there are valuable antiques, pictures, silver or jewellery an expert valuation is not necessary, and the executors should use their own knowledge and common sense. If in doubt a local valuator or auctioneer should be asked to inspect and value. He will only charge a modest fee for this service. The value the contents of a house are insured for is not a good guide, as this is (or should be) based on the cost of replacement, not what the items are worth.

A car is usually listed separately and described by its make and registration number. A good enough value can be obtained by seeing what prices are being asked for comparable cars in newspaper advertisements. Another method is to look up publications (such as *Glass's Guide*) which give the current values of second-hand cars. A proper inspection and valuation by a motor engineer should not be necessary.

Premium bonds, National Savings certificates and S.A.Y.E. contracts

Premium bonds are entered in the inventory at their face value. Any prizes won before the date of death that had not been paid to the deceased form part of his estate. National Savings certificates and Save As You Earn contracts, however, earn interest and the appropriate Government department will supply the date of death values on request. Enquiries should also be made to check that any such items were in name of the deceased and that he did not have any other holdings.

Shares

If the share certificates are among the deceased's papers then a list can be made up without any difficulty. A copy of his last income tax return (if available) will show what dividends etc. have been received and therefore what investments the deceased held. If the certificates can't be found at home the bank or the deceased's lawyer probably have them in safe custody. Shares in public companies that are quoted on the Stock Exchange can be valued by looking at the daily range of prices quoted for the date of death in *The Financial Times* or *Stock Exchange Gazette* and taking a "middle price". Even so the best way is to ask a stockbroker to value them for a small fee. Shares in private or non-quoted companies are more difficult to value and the usual method of valuation is to write to the company itself.

Insurance policies

The policies, receipts for premiums or bank statements showing premiums paid should alert executors to the existence of these items. As bonuses may be payable the executors should write to the insurance company for a note of the precise sum payable under each policy.

Sums due from employers

If the deceased was employed there is probably some pay due to the date of death, as most people are paid in arrears. There might also be accrued holiday pay. The employer should be asked to provide a statement of the sums due as well as a statement of the total pay and tax deducted in the current tax year. Many firms operate pension schemes which provide for quite large sums to be paid to an employee's estate if he dies before retirement. If the death occurred after retirement the widow(er) may become entitled to a pension, although such a pension is normally not part of the deceased's estate.

Income tax rebate

A person is entitled to his full personal allowance even if he dies half way through a tax year. Tax is deducted from pay on the basis that the person will live for the whole year so that there is often a refund of tax due. It is impossible to estimate the amount due and the Inland Revenue cannot provide a figure immediately. The rebate should be entered in the inventory at a nominal figure of £1. It should not be forgotten as the Inland Revenue may refuse to pay if this item was omitted from the confirmation. If they refuse to pay, an additional confirmation for this item will be necessary.

Gifts

If the deceased made substantial gifts before he died then these might have to be included as well. Gifts made before March 1974 and within 7 years of death must be included. Gifts made after March 1974 and within 3 years of death must also be notified to the Capital Taxes Office as more tax may be due on them.

Other assets

It is impossible to give examples of all the sorts of property that the deceased might have owned. The items given above are only the commonest items. If the deceased was self-employed then the value of the business (or his share in it) will have to be worked out. An accountant is nearly always needed to do this. The deceased may have been getting money from a family trust. Here again valuation of his interest is a skilled job.

12

Debts

As well as listing all the property of the deceased, his debts must be investigated and listed as well. Firstly, there is the funeral account and any medical or nursing expenses. Secondly, sums may be due to people like the local newsagent, grocer or milkman as well as other tradesmen for goods or services supplied but not paid for before death. If the house is rented there may be arrears of rent and rates due, while if it is owned there may be a substantial sum due to the building society or other lender. All these creditors should be asked to send in their bills or a note of the amount due. Don't forget the Inland Revenue. There may be a year or two's tax outstanding particularly if the deceased was in business. As explained later (page 41) many debts are not immediately payable.

If the deceased was in business there may be a lot of trade creditors. It can take a long time to make a complete list of these, and it might be worth advertising in the local newspapers or trade journals. This should also be done if there is any suspicion that the deceased had been in financial difficulties. It is most important that executors or relatives should not carry on the deceased's business in a spirit of helpfulness after his death if there is a possibility that the business is bankrupt. If they do they will become personally responsible for the deceased's business debts.

In general, only the deceased's property is liable for his debts. If there is not enough to pay everybody then creditors may only get paid a fraction of the amounts due to them. Other people can be held liable for the deceased's debts if they had agreed to be liable or were guarantors or carried on an insolvent business (see above). As an exception to this general rule funeral expenses can be recovered from a surviving spouse and parents are liable for their children's funeral expenses if the local authority carry out the funeral.

Some housing authorities ask a surviving spouse to pay off any arrears of rent at least when he or she had been living with the deceased tenant. This practice is of doubtful legality but if the surviving spouse wishes to stay on in the house, he or she has little option but to comply with the demand at present. The Tenants' Rights, Etc. (Scotland) Bill, currently being discussed in Parliament, will give the surviving spouse a right to take over the tenancy. The housing authority will no longer be able to make the transfer conditional on payment of arrears of rent due by the deceased tenant.

When debts exceed the value of the estate

An estate is insolvent where the debts and expenses due exceed the value of the property left. When this is discovered the executor should take legal advice immediately and meanwhile take no further steps in dealing with the property or towards obtaining confirmation. The creditors are informed of the situation and are left to take what steps they think fit.

OBTAINING CONFIRMATION

The executor who has been appointed to distribute the deceased's property must be officially approved before he can start. This approval is called confirmation because the sheriff confirms the executor who has been appointed by the will or appointed by the court previously.

Before the executor has been confirmed he should confine himself to safeguarding and collecting together the deceased's property. Valuables should be removed from an empty house and taken to a bank and the house made safe against intruders. It may be difficult to stop members of the family or others taking items which they are to get under the will, but the executor should be firm. He could be liable for anything missing if he fails to take steps to prevent such actions.

Any person who meddles with the deceased's property may be liable for all his debts if the deceased turns out to have been bankrupt. He may also be guilty of theft if he has no right under the will to any of the property he takes. Provided the executor is confirmed and acts prudently and within the scope of his duty, he does not incur liability for debts beyond the value of the estate. He should not dispose of any property before confirmation.

Confirmation to ordinary estates

(a) The inventory

The full list of the deceased's property is set out on a special form called a Capital Transfer Tax Form A-3. This form may be obtained from the Capital Taxes Office in Edinburgh or from main Post Offices. All property in the United Kingdom together with foreign moveable estate (see glossary) goes into the inventory proper. Foreign land goes into a different part of the form. There are also separate parts for gifts made by the deceased before death, land passing under a survivorship destination (see page 54), and trust property in which the deceased had an interest.

A solicitor usually completes this form from information supplied to him by the executor, but it is possible for an executor to complete the form himself, with assistance from the Capital Taxes Office or sheriff court staff.

The executor must take an oath that the information set out in the form is complete and accurate. This oath is sworn before a notary public, a justice of the peace or a sheriff. It is a serious offence knowingly to make false statements. Where the executor has been appointed by will he must swear to this as well as to the form. In the case of a holograph will (see page 52) two people who knew the deceased and his handwriting must testify to the genuineness of the document. Each of them must examine the will and swear (before a notary public etc.) a statement that in his opinion the will is genuine. The executor takes along these two sworn statements together with the holograph will.

(b) Payment of capital transfer tax

If capital transfer tax is due this must be paid before confirmation can be obtained. The tax is paid by sending off the completed form A-3 to the Capital Taxes Office in Edinburgh together with a cheque for the amount due. The solicitor will work out how much is due or the Capital Taxes Office will advise the executor. At this stage the amount payable is only provisional, as the value of some items may be altered or additional property subsequently discovered. Since the executors cannot touch any of the deceased's property before confirmation, they usually have to get a temporary loan in order to pay the tax. The deceased's bank manager is usually quite ready to lend the money required and arranging this is part of the service provided by a solicitor. The interest charged on the loan is payable out of the estate.

Where the estate is valued at less than the capital transfer tax exemption limit (currently £25,000 but an increase to £50,000 was proposed in the 1980 budget) the form (A-3) can be lodged for confirmation (see below) without being sent to the Capital Taxes Office beforehand. In certain circumstances tax may be due even though the estate is below the exemption limit. The sheriff clerks (and the Commissary Office) send copies of all inventories to the Capital Taxes Office so that they can check the tax position on inventories which have not been submitted to them first.

(c) Lodging the form for confirmation

The final step is to lodge (usually by post) the form (A-3) with the sheriff clerk of the sheriff court of the district in which the deceased was domiciled (see glossary). The Commissary Office in Edinburgh deals with all confirmations where the deceased was domiciled in Edinburgh, where the deceased was domiciled outwith Scotland but left property in Scotland, or where the deceased was domiciled in Scotland but had no domicile in any particular part of it. This last category includes people with no permanent residence and people who worked and died abroad, but who still retained their Scottish domicile. The will (if any) is also lodged, together with the two sworn statements in the case of a holograph will (see page 52).

An executor who has been appointed by the court will have to provide a guarantee that he will carry out his duties properly and that any losses will be made good. The guarantee is called a bond of caution (pronounced "kayshun") and is lodged along with the form. It can be obtained from any reputable insurance company on payment of a modest premium, the precise amount depending on the gross value of the estate. An executor who has been appointed by the deceased in his will does not have to provide a guarantee, as the law assumes that the deceased chose a trustworthy person to act as his executor.

A fee, called dues of confirmation, is charged for issuing confirmation. It has to be paid when the form is lodged with the sheriff clerk or the Commissary Office. The amount payable depends on the total value of the property in the United Kingdom. The dues of confirmation currently payable for an estate valued at £5,000 are £19.50 and for an estate valued at £25,000 are £50.25. These dues should be remembered when asking for a bank overdraft to cover tax and expenses payable before confirmation, as bank managers do not like people to exceed the arranged drawing limits.

After a few days the confirmation is issued and the will, if any, is returned. A confirmation shows the name and address of the deceased, who his executor is and a complete list of all the property photocopied from the inventory. Although the inventory may contain foreign moveable estate this is for tax purposes and the confirmation only confers authority on the executor to deal with property in the United Kingdom. The executor will have to take legal proceedings abroad to obtain authority to deal with any foreign property.

The confirmation needs to be shown to everybody who holds money or other assets which belonged to the deceased as evidence of the executor's right to demand and receive payment. Where the estate consists of many items it takes a long time to send the confirmation to each body in turn. To speed up the administration of an estate a separate certificate of confirmation (current cost 50p each) can be obtained for each item. These can be sent out to the various bodies simultaneously.

Confirmation to Small Estates

For small estates confirmation can be obtained without the help of a solicitor. At present a small estate is one where the gross value is less than £3,000 *and* the net value is less than £1,000. When the Confirmation to Small Estates (Scotland) Act 1979 is brought into operation on 1 July 1980, estates where the gross value does not exceed £10,000 will be classed as small. The gross value is the total value of the property without subtracting the debts. Instead of employing a solicitor the executor can take along the will, together with a list of the deceased's property and its value, to the sheriff court or Commissary Office. The clerk there will complete the necessary forms without additional charge and issue confirmation.

This procedure can also be used where no will has been left. The person entitled to be appointed executor (see page 6) goes along to the sheriff court or Commissary Office with a list of the property. Particulars are taken and an appointment made for the executor to return to sign the completed forms. A bond of caution (see page 15) from an insurance company is required before confirmation can be issued and advice is given on how to obtain a bond. At the second visit the executor takes along the bond of caution and two witnesses who swear to his identity and relationship to the deceased.

Executors using the small estates procedure must go to the sheriff court or Commissary Office themselves, together with the two witnesses where necessary. Only where the executor lives in England or Wales can he apply by post.

The small estates procedure avoids solicitors' charges for preparing the inventory and obtaining confirmation. Executors, however, still have to interpret the will (if there is one), list and value the deceased's property, collect it in and distribute it to those legally entitled to it. Most executors prefer to ask a solicitor to handle the whole business for them. It is estimated that in only 5-10% of small estates is use made of sheriff clerks.

Payment made without confirmation being required

Many bodies may pay up to £1,500 due to a beneficiary under a will, or a person entitled by law if there is no will, without the need for confirmation. These bodies include the National Savings Bank and other National Savings departments, Trustee Savings Banks, Friendly Societies (some of which are insurance companies) and the Armed Forces. Before payment can be made, the applicant must send the death certificate, a copy of the will (if any) or proof of his relationship to the deceased, and proof of his own identity.

Where the deceased nominated money to a person, i.e. specified who should get money or benefits due to him after his death (see page 54), that person can receive payment on proof of the death and proof of his identity. Confirmation is not needed and the sum can be paid over immediately after death. If the deceased left nothing except nominations or money with any of the above organisations, the trouble and expense of confirmation can be saved.

COLLECTING IN THE ESTATE

After confirmation the executor can start to collect in all the items of property which belonged to the deceased. Any money collected or received from the sale of various items should be put into a new bank account opened for this purpose. On no account should executors place this money in their own bank accounts. Sums (over say £50) that are not required immediately should be placed in a deposit account where they will earn interest. Executors should not speculate or invest the money in other ways. Only if there is a trust set up by the will may the trustees (who are usually the executors as well) make investments. There may be restrictions as to what investments are allowed, and in every case proper advice from a stockbroker should be taken beforehand.

The executor or the lawyer sends the confirmation (or certificates of confirmation) to all the bodies holding money or property that belonged to the deceased asking for it to be handed over. A few examples of typical

E

17

items will show what is involved. This stage of collecting all the estate can take several months if there are many items.

Money in the Bank, Building Society or other Accounts

The branch concerned should be written to, enclosing the confirmation and requesting payment. If there is a pass-book this should be enclosed as well. After a few days a cheque for the balance due and interest (if any) to date of payment will be sent and the confirmation and pass-book returned. Some bodies like the Trustee Savings Bank insist on a formal receipt being signed by the executor before they will pay out.

House

(a) Rented houses

If the house was rented from a local authority or housing association, they should be notified of the tenant's death. The Tenants' Rights, Etc. (Scotland) Bill currently being discussed in Parliament will allow the widow(er) or another member of the family (over 16) who had lived in the home to take over the tenancy, or to stay there for up to three months after the death if they do not wish to take over the tenancy. The Bill also prevents a local authority or housing association from requiring the deceased tenant's family to move to a smaller house.

Where the house is rented from a private landlord, he should be informed of the death and whether the widow(er) or other member of the family (including an unmarried partner) of the deceased wish to exercise their right to stay on. Some tenancies (especially of farms) can be bequeathed by will or transferred to a member of the deceased tenant's family when there is no will. Legal advice should be taken in these cases to ensure that the correct procedure is followed.

If nobody wants to remain in the house, then it should be emptied and the keys handed in as soon as possible, otherwise rent and rates will continue to be charged. A service tenancy i.e. a tenancy tied to employment terminates on the death of the employee, so that his family has no right to remain in the house.

(b) Owned houses

If the house is to be taken over by a beneficiary then the title has to be made over to that person. This is not necessary where the property passes automatically to the survivor in a survivorship destination (see page 54). If the house is to be sold it should be put on the market as soon as possible to prevent costly maintenance and possible vandalism. Selling a house is not an easy task. Executors are well advised to consult a solicitor right at the start, even though his services are only strictly necessary to prepare and register the documents of title.

Where there is an outstanding loan over the house, the building society or other lender should be told what arrangements are being made to pay back the loan. Sometimes loan agreements have linked life insurance policies which provide money to pay back the loan on the premature death of the borrower. Otherwise a building society will often agree to the loan being continued by the member of the family taking over the house. A solicitor will however have to prepare a new security document in this case.

Furniture and Contents of the House

No formal steps are necessary to take possession of furniture and contents which are already in the house. For articles held by other people a request for their delivery should be made accompanied by the confirmation. If there are still payments to be made on hire-purchase goods the executor should enquire into the position as soon as possible after death before arrears mount up. Some hire-purchase agreements have provisions in them cancelling the debt on the death of the purchaser. The supplier should not be allowed to take the goods back before legal advice has been taken on whether he is entitled to do so. If there are any valuables it could be a good idea for these to be stored temporarily in a safe or with a bank, but it is important not to forget about them when the estate comes to be distributed.

Insurance Policies

The policy and the confirmation should be sent to the insurance company, together with an extract certificate of death. If the policy has been lost the company will still pay provided the policy is in force and all the premiums have been paid. The company will usually require the executor to sign a receipt before making payment. The amount stated in the receipt should be checked carefully before signing.

Shares

The share certificates and the confirmation are sent to the companies requesting the death to be noted and the certificates to be endorsed with the executor's name. When this is done future dividends will be paid to the executor. He can then sell the shares or make them over to one of the beneficiaries. Where the actual certificate cannot be found, the company will issue a new certificate in name of the executor if he obtains an indemnity from a bank, guaranteeing to make good any loss if the original certificate turns up. This is not expensive.

Sums due from Employers

There are usually arrears of pay (and accrued holiday pay) due, but there may also be money from pension funds. A request for payment accompanied by the confirmation should be made to the employer. Sums due under pension schemes are paid by the pension fund trustees (usually an insurance company) rather than by the employer, and a similar request for payment should be made to them.

Compensation for death

Damages can be claimed if the deceased's death was caused by somebody's negligence or failure to carry out their legal duty. Apart from this, the Criminal Injuries Compensation Board will make payments to the widow(er) and dependants, where the deceased was the victim of a violent crime or where his injuries were sustained in preventing a crime or hindering the criminals. In both cases legal advice should be sought to decide whether a claim is worth pursuing.

Benefits and allowances for the family

Benefits and allowances payable by the Department of Health and Social Security to the deceased's family after his death do not (with the exception of death grant (see page 4)) form part of his estate. They can be an important source of income for the family. The executor or solicitor should at least inform the surviving spouse about these as part of his responsibility for looking after the family's financial affairs.

A widow may be entitled to a widow's allowance, a widowed mother's allowance, or a widow's pension. The amount payable depends on her husband's record of National Insurance contributions. They are payable whether the widow has a job or not, but they are taxable and cease when the widow remarries or lives with a man as if she were married. If the husband's death was due to service in the armed forces then a war widow's pension is payable, while if death resulted from an industrial accident or disease, industrial death benefit can be claimed. A supplement to any existing child benefit is payable on becoming a widow. The local Social Security office will provide further information and will help with claiming any benefit due.

If the family is left without any income after the death of a breadwinner supplementary benefit can be claimed. The family may also become eligible for rent or rates rebates. The local Social Security office should be informed of the death and the payment books should be returned if the deceased was in receipt of any state benefits. A supplementary pension book held by a husband in respect of his wife must be returned to the Social Security office for alteration immediately on her death. It is an offence for any person to cash benefits to which he or she is no longer entitled.

FIRST STEPS IN DEALING WITH AN ESTATE

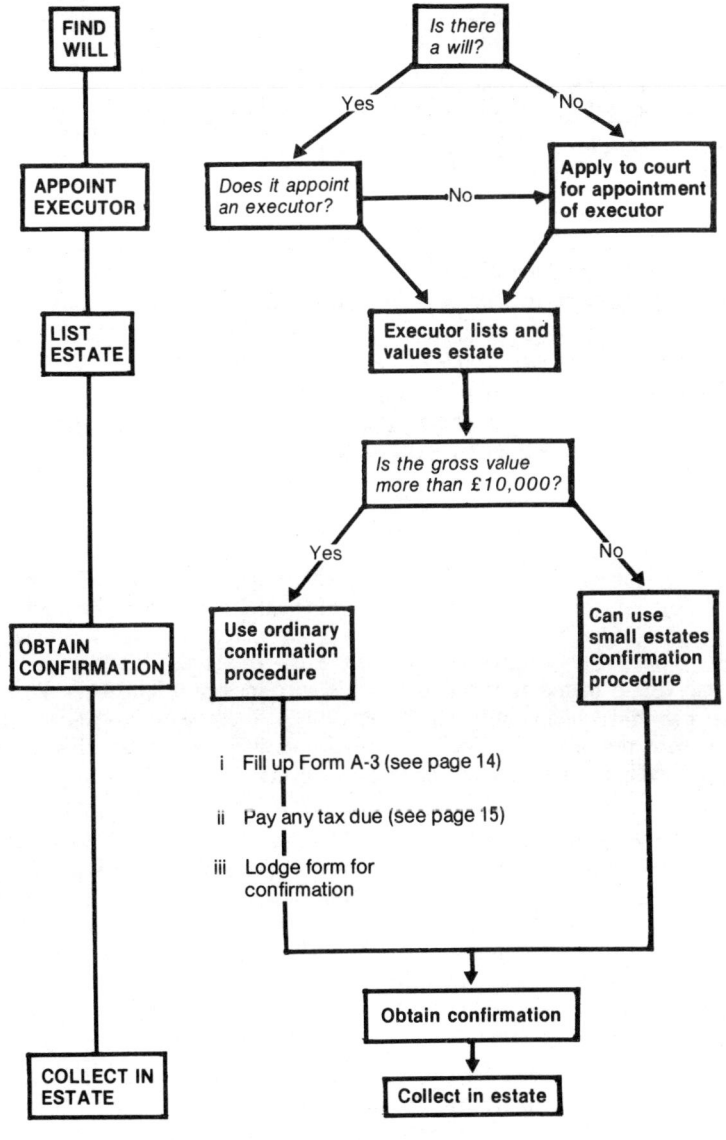

FIND WILL

APPOINT EXECUTOR

LIST ESTATE

OBTAIN CONFIRMATION

COLLECT IN ESTATE

Is there a will?

Yes — No

Does it appoint an executor? — No → Apply to court for appointment of executor

Executor lists and values estate

Is the gross value more than £10,000?

Yes — No

Use ordinary confirmation procedure

Can use small estates confirmation procedure

i   Fill up Form A-3 (see page 14)

ii Pay any tax due (see page 15)

iii Lodge form for confirmation

Obtain confirmation

Collect in estate

CHAPTER 3

Rules of Inheritance when there is no Will: Intestate Succession

This chapter is directed at the executors who wish to understand how the estate should be divided up when there is no will (or there is property which the will has not dealt with), and to the relatives and friends who wish to understand what their rights of inheritance might be. It deals first with the "prior rights" of the surviving spouse and the "legal rights" of the spouse, children or grandchildren, and then with how the remainder of the property is distributed after prior and legal rights have been satisfied.

Introduction

Nearly two-thirds of all people dying in Scotland die without leaving a will (intestate). In order to prevent a free-for-all by relatives in such cases, legal rules govern the distribution of any property amongst the deceased's family. These rules apply not only where the deceased did not leave a will but also where property is left which his will does not deal with. Particular items may have been omitted, for example, or unlikely events may occur which were not provided for in the will. Any property not dealt with by will is called intestate property or intestate estate.

The law attempts to distribute the intestate property in much the same way as the deceased might have done had he left a will. Before 1964 the rules governing distribution were derived partly from feudal law and partly from the law of the Church. Any land and buildings usually went to a male descendant. All the other property was divided up among the rest of the family. This produced a result unfair to the surviving spouse and daughters. The Succession (Scotland) Act 1964 together with more recent amendments has replaced most of the old law and provides a much more socially acceptable scheme of division.

Briefly, the law provides first for the surviving spouse, whose rights, called prior rights, have priority over other claims. Next, the children and the surviving spouse are entitled to part of the moveable property (i.e. any property except land and buildings). Their rights are termed legal rights. Finally, the remainder of the property goes to the nearest relatives, the order being children and their descendants, parents and/or brothers and sisters (and their descendants), grand-parents, uncles and aunts and their descendants etc. If no relatives, however remote, can be found then the property goes to the Crown. In practice, unless the deceased was rich, the surviving spouse will inherit all or most of the estate. Appendix III gives some worked examples of the operation of the legal rules.

PRIOR RIGHTS

The purpose of the prior rights is to ensure that the widow(er) is left with at least a furnished home to live in together with some money. It must be emphasised that these rights only arise when there is no will covering these items at least. These rights may only be claimed by a surviving *spouse*. A divorced wife is not entitled to any part of her ex-husband's unwilled property but a separated wife can still claim. A man or a woman who had been living with the deceased as if married may be able to claim. Provided the couple were free to marry (i.e. were not married to somebody else) and they had lived together for a considerable time, the survivor can obtain a statement called a declarator of marriage from the Court of Session, and is then treated as a spouse.

There are three separate rights involved in prior rights — the right to a house, the right to furniture and the right to money. The surviving spouse's prior rights are extremely valuable. Even where there are children the spouse is entitled to the house, furniture and plenishings and £8,000. Many of those who die without a will leave less than this. In these cases the widow(er) inherits the whole estate.

The home
The surviving spouse has a right to the house (or the share of the house) owned by the deceased if:
  (a) it is in Scotland;
  (b) it is worth less than £30,000; and
  (c) he or she was living in it at the date of death of the deceased.

If the house (or share of it) is worth more than £30,000 then the surviving spouse receives £30,000 in cash instead. Another case where the surviving spouse gets the money value (up to a limit of £30,000) is where the house forms part of a larger property which was used by the deceased for a business. Examples might be a farm and farm house or the owner's flat in a hotel. If the deceased owned more than one house and the surviving spouse lived in both for part of the time, he or she can choose which house to take. Usually the more valuable one is chosen.

Where the property is tenanted, prior rights give the surviving spouse the right to take over the remainder of the lease. Prior rights cannot, however, be claimed from a Rent Act tenancy, and in practice the absence of security of tenure in public sector tenancies renders prior rights to these worthless. For the surviving spouse's rights in these cases see page 10.

Furniture

A bare house is not much use to the surviving spouse. As refurnishing can be very expensive, he or she is entitled to all the furniture and plenishings in the house up to a value of £8,000. The furniture and plenishings must have belonged to the deceased and not been on hire-purchase. Furniture and plenishings means everything that one would normally expect to find in a house e.g. tables, chairs, beds, a television, a cooker, sofas, carpets, pictures, books, china, cutlery, and food and drink. Money and investments are not included nor is jewellery, as these are personal possessions rather than relating to the house. A car is not counted either. If the total value of the furniture and plenishings in the house is greater than £8,000 then a choice must be made of items up to this value.

The right to furniture is distinct from the right to the house. This means that if the house was tenanted or has been left to someone else, the surviving spouse can still claim the furniture if unwilled.

Money

The right of a surviving spouse to a sum of money is in addition to the right to a house and plenishings. Where the deceased was not survived by any of his children (including illegitimate or adopted children) or any of their legitimate or adopted descendants, the surviving spouse is entitled to £16,000. The survival of any children or their descendants restricts the spouse to the sum of £8,000.

Where only part of the deceased's property is not dealt with by his will, then if the surviving spouse receives a legacy (other than a house and plenishings), he or she cannot take the £16,000 or £8,000 in full out of any unwilled property. The value of the legacy must be deducted and only the balance (if any) is due.

LEGAL RIGHTS

The legal rights which may be claimed by a surviving spouse and children are very ancient in origin. They can only be claimed out of the moveable estate (i.e. everything except land and buildings). In this section legal rights when no will is left are discussed, but legal rights may also be claimed even when the deceased left a will (see page 38). The share of the moveable estate taken by a claimant depends on whether the deceased was survived by a spouse alone, descendants alone or both.

Descendants alone

If a person dies without leaving a surviving spouse, the children's legal rights (sometimes called legitim) amount to one-half of the moveable estate. The children normally share this equally (but see page 25 for exceptions). Children include illegitimate children of the deceased who can prove their relationship, and children adopted by the deceased. Step-children cannot claim legal rights as they are not offspring of the deceased.

Where a child dies before the deceased, then his or her legitimate or adopted children divide among them what would have been their parent's share. The spouse of the child has no claim however. If all the deceased's children have died beforehand the sum available for legal rights is shared equally among the surviving grandchildren. Legitimate or adopted children of a grandchild can take the share of the legal rights their parent would have had in his grandparent's estate.

The following example illustrates how children and grandchildren share the money available for legal rights.

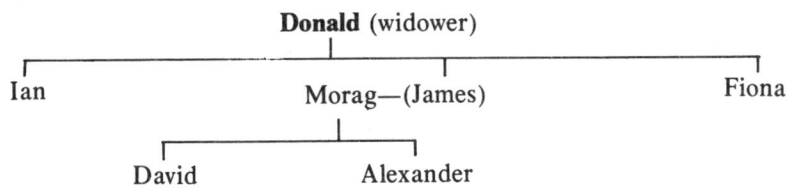

Donald dies without a will leaving £12,000 in various bank and building society accounts. His son James died in a car crash some years before. As Donald leaves no widow the children's legal rights amount to £6,000 (i.e. one half of £12,000). Ian and Fiona receive £2,000 each and the remaining £2,000, which would have gone to James had he survived, is divided among his sons David and Alexander equally (i.e. £1,000 each). James's widow Morag has no claim.

A child may renounce his legal rights while his parent is alive, perhaps in return for a gift. In this case he and his descendants do not count for the purpose of sharing out the money available under legal rights. In the above example if James had renounced his legal rights Ian and Fiona would divide the £6,000 equally between them, and David and Alexander would receive nothing. A child's share can also be affected if he was given money by his deceased parent to set him up in business or on his marriage.

Spouse alone

The surviving spouse's legal rights are in addition to prior rights. In the absence of any children (or their legitimate or adopted descendants) the surviving spouse's legal rights amount to one-half of the remainder of the moveable property after the furniture and plenishings (up to a value of £8,000) and £16,000 arising from prior rights have been deducted. Where the deceased left land and buildings in addition to the dwellinghouse, part of the £16,000 is deemed to have been taken from the other land and buildings, rather than totally from the moveable property. This makes the calculation of legal rights more complicated.

F

Spouse and children

Even when there are children (or their legitimate or adopted descendants) the surviving spouse's legal rights are in addition to prior rights. The legal rights of the surviving spouse amount to one-third of the remainder of the moveable property after the furniture and plenishings (up to a total of £8,000) and £8,000 arising from prior rights have been deducted. The legal rights of the children amount to another third. The money from legal rights is divided among the children (or their descendants) in the same way as described earlier (see page 24). Once again the position is more complex if the deceased owned land and buildings as well as a house.

The following example illustrates the working of legal rights when both a spouse and children survive.

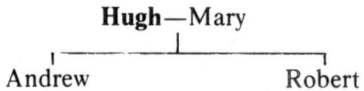

Hugh dies intestate leaving a house, furniture and plenishings and £14,000 in other moveable property. His widow Mary takes the house, furniture and plenishings and £8,000 as her prior rights. The balance of the moveable estate amounts to £6,000. Mary's legal rights are to £2,000 (i.e. one-third of £6,000), while another £2,000 is divided equally between the children Andrew and Robert.

REMAINDER OF THE PROPERTY

The remainder of the estate, after prior and legal rights (if any) have been met, goes to the deceased's nearest relatives. Where the deceased left neither spouse nor descendants the remainder of the estate is the whole estate. The order of claimants is (1) descendants, (2) brothers, sisters and parents, (3) spouse, (4) remoter relations and (5) the Crown.

(1) Descendants

The children, including illegitimate and adopted children, are the first claimants. They share the remainder equally, but legitimate and adopted grandchildren divide what would have been their dead parent's share. If all the children are dead the grandchildren share the remainder equally amongst themselves.

(2) Brothers, Sisters and Parents

If the deceased left no descendants then the remainder of the property is divided among his brothers and sisters together with his parents. Where the deceased's parents died before him, his brothers and sisters share the whole remainder equally between them. The children of a dead brother or sister can claim what would have been their parent's share. Half brothers and sisters only share when there are no full brothers or sisters or their descendants surviving. A child who has been jointly adopted by a couple is treated as a full brother or sister of any other child they adopt or of any child of their marriage. An illegitimate child has no right to share in his brothers' or sisters' property and *vice versa*.

Where there are no full or half brothers or sisters nor any of their descendants, the surviving parents share the remainder of the property. Where only one parent survives he or she takes the whole remainder. If the father of an illegitimate person is known then he should be informed of his rights, but extensive enquiries need not be made to find a father or to establish his paternity.

Where there are parents and brothers or sisters (or their descendants) then the parent or parents are entitled to half the remainder of the property, with the brothers or sisters (or their descendants) sharing the rest as outlined above.

(3) Spouse

The next person in line is the surviving spouse. If there are no descendants, brothers or sisters (or their descendants) or parents then the surviving spouse is entitled to the whole remainder of the property.

(4) Remoter relations

After the surviving spouse come uncles and aunts of the deceased and their descendants. Then grandparents, then great uncles and great aunts and their descendants and so on until hopefully someone is found to inherit the deceased's whole unwilled estate, as there can be no prior or legal rights in these cases.

(5) The Crown

If no relations can be traced then the Crown (i.e. the State) through an official called the Queen's and Lord Treasurer's Remembrancer takes the estate as ultimate heir. About 200 estates per year go to the Crown because no family can be found. After the debts and funeral expenses have been paid, the property is handed over to the Queen's and Lord Treasurer's Remembrancer, who will usually advertise this fact in local newspapers to alert possible claimants. If no family turns up to claim the property the Crown is prepared to make gifts to applicants who have moral but no legal claims to the property. Only a few (between 20 and 30) gifts by the Crown are made each year, usually to relatives of an illegitimate person who have no legal rights to his estate, or to close friends or neighbours who have rendered substantial services to the deceased without payment.

Adopted, illegitimate and step relationships

Although these have been mentioned in passing the rules for these relationships are summarised here.

(a) Illegitimate children

Before 1926 an illegitimate child had no claim on his parents' unwilled

I SPOUSE SURVIVING

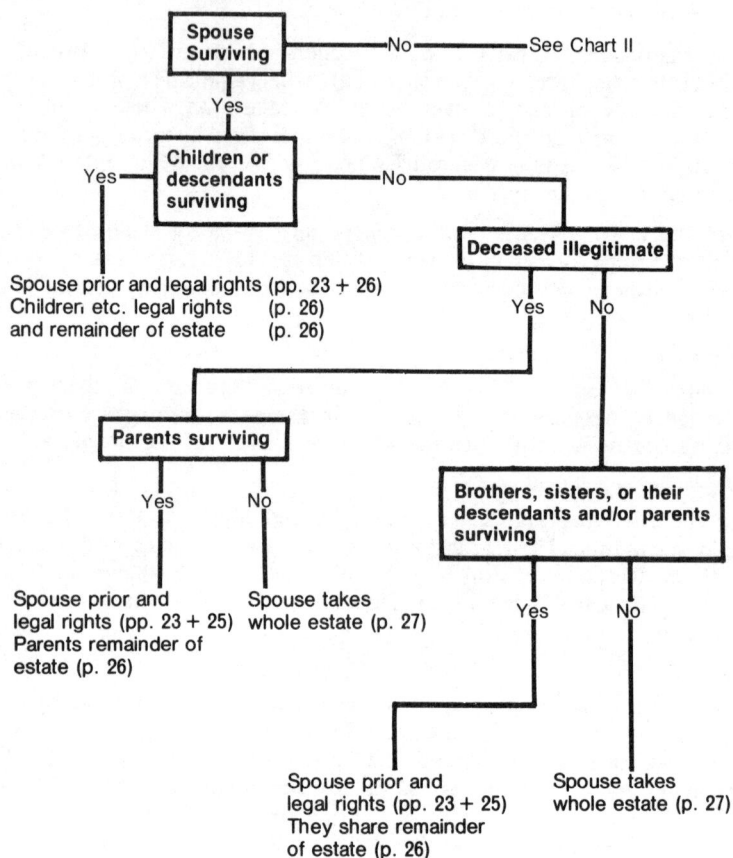

Spouse Surviving ──No── See Chart II

Yes

Children or descendants surviving

Yes

No

Spouse prior and legal rights (pp. 23 + 26)
Children etc. legal rights (p. 26)
and remainder of estate (p. 26)

Deceased illegitimate

Yes   No

Parents surviving

Yes   No

Spouse prior and
legal rights (pp. 23 + 25)
Parents remainder of
estate (p. 26)

Spouse takes
whole estate (p. 27)

Brothers, sisters, or their descendants and/or parents surviving

Yes   No

Spouse prior and
legal rights (pp. 23 + 25)
They share remainder
of estate (p. 26)

Spouse takes
whole estate (p. 27)

II NO SPOUSE SURVIVING

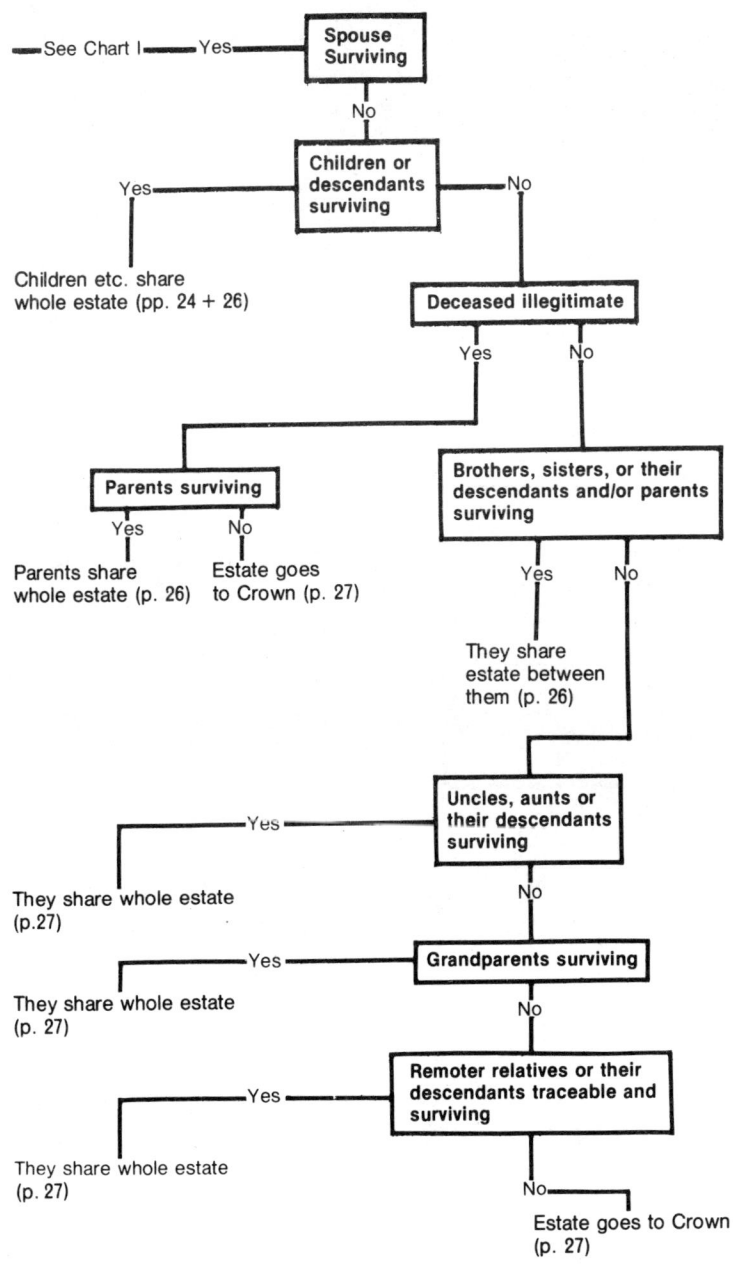

See Chart I — Yes —
Spouse Surviving
No

Children or descendants surviving
Yes — No

Children etc. share whole estate (pp. 24 + 26)

Deceased illegitimate
Yes — No

Parents surviving
Yes — No

Parents share whole estate (p. 26)

Estate goes to Crown (p. 27)

Brothers, sisters, or their descendants and/or parents surviving
Yes — No

They share estate between them (p. 26)

Uncles, aunts or their descendants surviving
Yes — No

They share whole estate (p.27)

Grandparents surviving
Yes — No

They share whole estate (p. 27)

Remoter relatives or their descendants traceable and surviving
Yes — No

They share whole estate (p. 27)

Estate goes to Crown (p. 27)

29

III DECEASED LEAVES SPOUSE AND CHILDREN

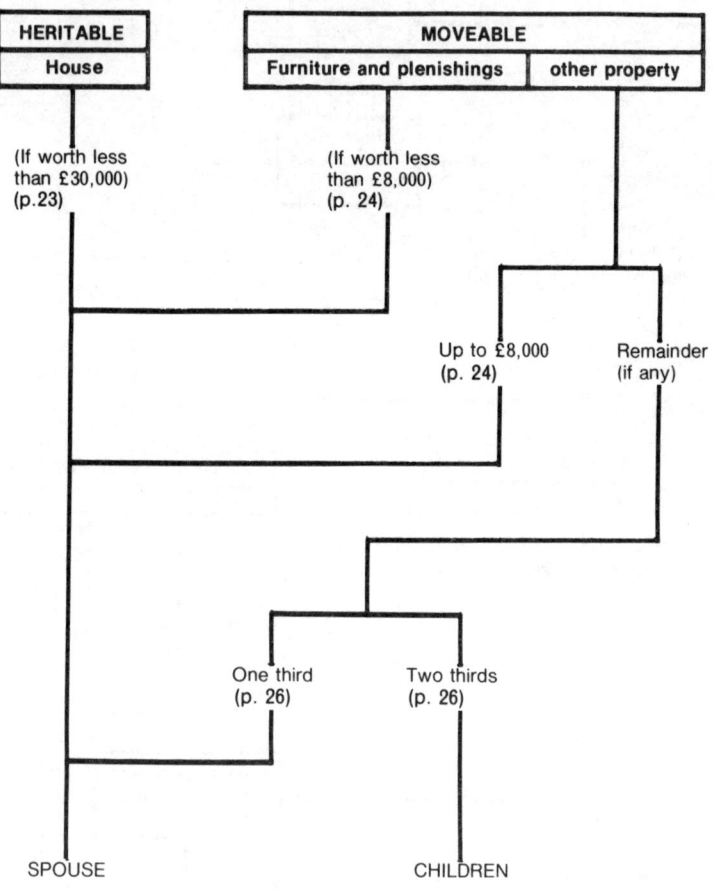

IV DECEASED LEAVES SPOUSE AND A BROTHER BUT NO DESCENDANTS

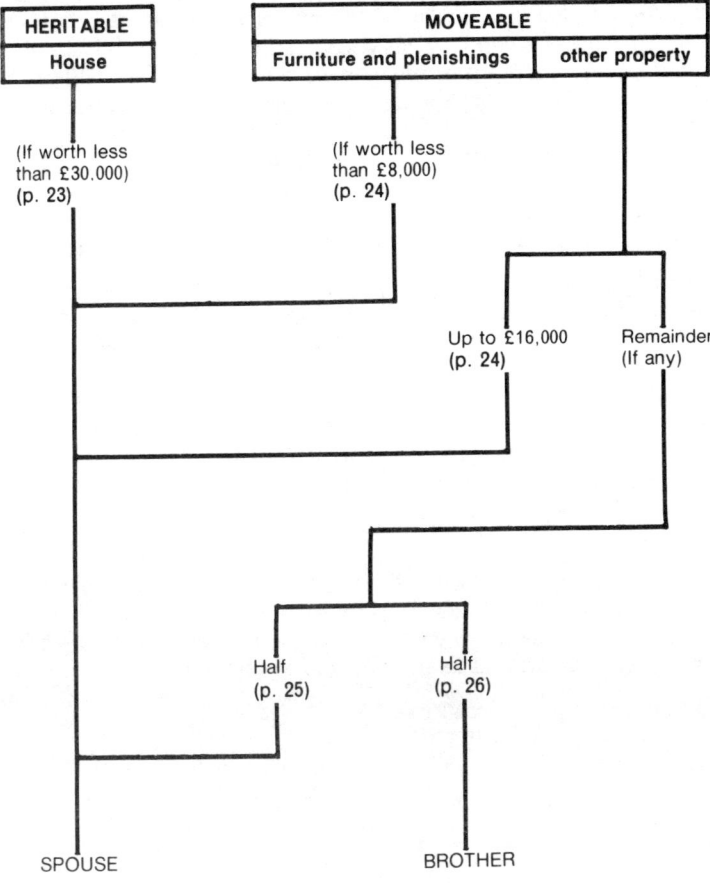

property, but in that year he was given limited rights to his mother's property if she died without a will. Since 25th November 1968 an illegitimate child has a claim on both his parents' unwilled property. He cannot, however, claim a share to any of his grandparents', brothers' or sisters' or any other remoter relatives' unwilled property. If the deceased was himself illegitimate, the only people who have a legal claim on his unwilled property are his spouse, his descendants (except illegitimate grandchildren and remoter descendants with an illegitimate link) and his parents. If he was not survived by any of these relations then his estate goes to the Crown. Brothers and sisters and other relations can, however, apply to the Queen's and Lord Treasurer's Remembrancer for a gift of part of his property, provided they can establish their relationship.

(b) Adopted children

Adopted children used to have no rights in their adoptive parents' unwilled property for they retained their rights to their natural parents' estates. Since 10th September 1964 a child who has been jointly adopted by a couple is treated as their legitimate child, and as a full brother or sister of any other child they adopt or any child of their marriage. A child who is adopted by a single person is treated as the legitimate child of that person, and as a half brother or sister to any other children whether natural or adopted of that person.

(c) Stepchildren

Stepchildren, being children of the deceased's spouse by a former marriage, have no direct relationship with the deceased. They have no right to any part of his unwilled property, even though they may have been brought up since babyhood as members of his family.

CHAPTER 4

Rules of Inheritance when there is a Will: Testate Succession

This chapter is again directed at the executors and possible beneficiaries. It discusses various complications which may affect distribution according to a will such as the possible invalidity of the will, changes in circumstances since the will was written, and what happens if the estate is insufficient to pay all legacies. The chapter discusses the "legal rights" of the surviving spouse and children, that is their right to make certain claims in preference to accepting any legacy made in their favour.

Challenging a will

A will or part of it may be challenged on many grounds. Legal proceedings in the Court of Session are necessary in every case since a will which appears valid stands until it is declared void (see glossary). It is up to the challengers to prove their case, except where the genuineness of a holograph will (see page 52) is disputed. If the estate is not large, challenging may not be worth while, as the legal expenses can be considerable. See Appendix VI for Legal Aid.

(a) Forgery

For a will to be valid it must be signed by the person making it. Proof of forgery may be difficult as the only evidence may be opinions of handwriting experts and a person's writing often changes in his last years of life.

(b) Force and fear

A will is void if violence or threats of violence were used to induce the deceased to make a will against his wishes.

(c) Facility and circumvention

Nearly everybody in a family tends consciously or unconsciously to press their claims on a relative making a will. As long as the person has a strong mind almost any influence short of force and fear will not invalidate his will. A person with a weak or irresolute mind (facile) can be much more easily persuaded (circumvented) to make a will against his usual wishes. It is difficult to draw the line between legitimate advice or suggestions and schemes to bend a facile person's mind. Successful challenges on the ground of facility and circumvention have occurred where the person was senile, completely under the control of a particular relative, or not in receipt of independent advice.

(d) Misrepresentation

A will or a particular provision in it may be challenged if the person making it had been under a misapprehension brought about by false statements. A completely new will may have been signed under the mistaken belief that it merely made minor changes to an existing will. Another example would be where a man said his sister had died and their mother then changed her will leaving all her money to him.

(e) Uncertainty

A legacy is void if it is impossible to decide either what is given or the person to whom it is given (see page 59). A trust (see page 50) will be void if its purposes are uncertain, but provided the purposes are clear the court will supply any missing administrative details.

(f) Contrary to public policy

A particular gift in a will can be challenged if it confers no benefit on anybody. The classic example of a provision in a will which conferred no benefit occurred in the McCaig case in the early part of this century. Mr McCaig when alive built the large tower in Oban, which still dominates the town. Under his will it was to be made into a private mausoleum and furnished with enormous bronze statues of himself and his family. The court decided that such a provision was void. A person is allowed to leave a small sum for the erection of a headstone and upkeep of his grave, but an excessive sum to provide for fresh flowers every week would be regarded as a waste of money.

(g) Will improperly executed
(see pages 51 and 52).

(h) Will made by a person under age
(see page 49).

(i) Will made by an insane person
(see page 49).

(j) Children born afterwards
(see page 37).

A will cannot be challenged because a witness receives a legacy or some other benefit under the will.

Beneficiaries dying beforehand or ceasing to exist

A beneficiary must survive the deceased before he or she is entitled to the legacy. If he or she dies beforehand the legacy goes to someone else or becomes unwilled property. A well-thought-out will takes into account the possibility of a beneficiary dying beforehand and will provide for an alternative beneficiary. For example, the deceased might leave "£1,000 to my nephew Ian Smith, whom failing to his wife Agnes McDougal or Smith". Provided Ian is alive at the date of death of the deceased, he is entitled to the £1,000. If not, Agnes will inherit, provided she in turn is alive. It is impossible to provide for every contingency. The whole family may be wiped out in an air crash. It is only sensible, however, to make alternative provisions for the residue or for other substantial legacies especially where a beneficiary, because of his age or ill-health, could well fail to survive.

Occasionally, when a beneficiary dies beforehand, the legacy may, by a legal rule, go to his children even though they are not mentioned in the will. The beneficiary must have been a child, grandchild, nephew or niece of the deceased, but even here the rule cannot be relied on, as it depends on the whole scheme of the will and its precise wording. If children are intended to take their deceased parent's share, this should be stated clearly in the will.

A legacy may be left to more than one person. For example, the deceased may leave his house to two of his friends. If one of them dies before the deceased, the other will inherit the whole property. There are two exceptions to this rule. First, as explained in the preceding paragraph, a share may pass to children. Second, where the will said the legacy was to be shared equally by named individuals (but not by a group such as children or nieces), each person is only entitled to their original share.

Where a charity named in the will has ceased to exist, the legacy may be paid to another charity with similar aims rather than allowed to lapse. A court authorises this arrangement.

Simultaneous deaths

Where two people die in a road accident or other disaster and there is no evidence to indicate the order of death, it is presumed that the younger survived the elder. Thus, where a father and daughter die in an air crash the daughter will inherit anything left to her by her father and this, together with the daughter's own property, passes to her heirs. The major exception to this rule concerns a married couple. The presumption here is that they died simultaneously. Each spouse's property is distributed as if the other had failed to survive.

Insufficient estate to pay all the legacies

If the debts exceed the total value of the property left these must be paid as far as possible (see page 41) and there will be nothing left to pay the legacies. However the property left may be sufficient to pay all the debts and expenses but not to pay all the legacies. It is then a question of deciding how much each beneficiary is to receive. Unless the will says what is to happen in this situation, and that is very rare, the sharing out is governed by legal rules, as follows.

Debts, expenses and taxes are paid first. Next come special legacies. These are particular items like a car, jewellery, or all the premium bonds owned by the deceased. If these are still in existence at the date of death then they are handed over to the beneficiaries, unless they must be sold in order to provide money to pay the debts. After special legacies come general legacies. These are gifts of money or part of a number of similar objects owned by the deceased, e.g. sheep. General legacies are paid only where there is something left after payment of debts, expenses, taxes and the special legacies. If there is insufficient to pay all the general legacies in full, each beneficiary will only get a proportion of his general legacy. Residue is the last in the queue. A person who has been left the residue or remainder of the estate only gets what (if anything) is left after paying all the debts, expenses, taxes, special and general legacies in full.

Example

A woman leaves property worth £4,500. She bequeaths £1,500 to her sister (general legacy), her car (worth £1,500) to her son (special legacy) and the residue of her estate (£1,500) to her husband, who does not wish to claim legal rights (see page 38). If the total debts etc. come to £500 her son gets the car, her sister gets £1,500 but her husband only gets £1,000. If the total debts etc. come to £2,000 her son gets the car, her sister gets £1,000 while her husband gets nothing. Finally, if the debts etc. amount to £4,000 both the husband and sister get nothing. The son receives £500, being the balance left after the car has been sold in order to meet the debts.

Loss of special legacies

A special legacy is a legacy of a specific item such as a ring, furniture or a house. It is handed over to the beneficiary if it still belonged to the deceased at the date of his death, unless it must be sold to meet the debts. If the ring had been lost or the furniture had been given away before death, then the beneficiary gets nothing.

An error which often occurs in home-made wills results in a legacy of a house lapsing. If the house is described in the will by its address, unless the will is altered after a move the beneficiary will not receive it, because the house described in the will no longer belongs to the deceased. This unfortunate result can be avoided by altering the will after each move or, by adding after the address of the house, the phrase "or such other house as I may own."

More than one will left

Two (or more) wills may be left. This situation often happens when a person makes a home-made will and forgets another will made perhaps years ago. Both wills are valid, unless the later one revokes or cancels (see page 55) the earlier one, but if there is any conflict between the two then the provisions in the later one prevail. If the first will gave a watch to a daughter, while the second will gave it to a son the son would be entitled to the watch. Another example would be the gift of a grandfather clock in the second will, which overrides a gift of the whole furniture to somebody else in the first will.

Another problem that can arise when there are two valid wills is that the same person may have been left legacies in each of them. Even where the legacies are exactly the same, it is presumed that the person was intended to have both.

Loss of a will

A will is an extremely valuable document and every effort should be made to keep it safe with other important papers, either at home, at a bank, or with the lawyer who prepared it. If a will has been lost or destroyed by accident then a copy or even a draft can be declared equivalent to the original by the Court of Session. This is an expensive process (£300 or upwards). The will is treated as if it had never been made if it has been deliberately destroyed or if no copies or drafts survive. Where a person is known to have had his will and it cannot be found after his death, it is presumed that he destroyed it because he changed his mind and no longer wished it to be effective. Only where it can be shown that the destruction was accidental, or done under a misapprehension, can any copy in this case be declared equivalent to the missing original.

Effect of birth of children, marriage or divorce on a will

Scots law presumes that where a child or further children are born after a will which fails to provide for them has been made, a reasonable parent would wish to make a new will to include the addition(s) to his family. If death occurs before this can be done the child(ren) born after the will can ask the Court of Session to set aside the will. A challenge will fail if it is clear that the parent decided not to alter his will as he never intended the later child(ren) to benefit. The decision to challenge or not is for the child(ren) alone. It may be better financially to let the will stand and claim legal rights instead (see page 38).

A will made before marriage is not revoked by the marriage. Although the spouse can claim legal rights (see page 38), this is not usually a satisfactory substitute for a will that makes proper provision for him or her. Anybody who has already made a will should on getting married (or remarried) make a new will. Another reason for making a new will on marriage is to provide for any step-children. Unless they are specifically included in the will they cannot benefit. Step-children are not included in the term "children" (see page 58), nor can they claim legal rights (see page 38).

Divorce does not invalidate a will either. Unless a new will is made the ex-spouse may continue to benefit and if this happens the new spouse receives nothing. Although legal rights may be claimed by the disappointed new spouse, this is not usually a satisfactory substitute.

Jointly owned property: survivorship destinations

A survivorship destination in a title to land exists if the title transfers the property on death from the joint owners to the survivor when one dies (see page 54). It depends on how the property was paid for whether either of the joint owners can make different arrangements in their wills. Where both helped pay for the property, this usually prevents either of them cancelling the destination to the survivor and leaving their share to anybody else. On the other hand, if only one of the owners paid for the property, he can leave his share to whomever he likes, but the other owner cannot will away his share at all. Any provision in a will that is contrary to these rules is invalid.

Supposing a joint owner is entitled to cancel a survivorship destination and wishes to leave his share to somebody else. Since 1964 he can only cancel it by specifically referring to it and expressly cancelling it. Thus he would have to say in his will "I revoke the destination contained in the disposition by (name of the seller) in favour of myself and my wife and the survivor dated 15 May 1979" or similar words. If left uncancelled, the survivorship destination remains effective and overrules any other disposal of the property made by the deceased's will. The property may, however, be required to meet the deceased's debts.

Money or benefits: nominations

Money held by various bodies, e.g. National Savings Bank, may be nominated (see page 54) by the deceased to a person rather than leaving it to that person by will. A nomination cannot be cancelled in a later will but must be cancelled by notifying the organisation. The organisation should be written to for a special form for cancelling a nomination. The form should be completed in accordance with any accompanying instructions and returned. A copy or note of the form should be kept so that executors are aware the nomination has been cancelled. Unless the nomination is cancelled, the money goes to the nominee even though it has been left to someone else by will. The nominee may have to hand over the money to the executor if it is required to pay debts or legal rights.

LEGAL RIGHTS WHEN THERE IS A WILL

Most people provide as well as they can for their wife or husband and children in their wills. If they do not, these relatives can claim part of the estate. A claim for legal rights is a claim for a sum of money and not for any specific items that belong to the deceased. Because legal rights can only be claimed out of moveable property they may not be worth very much since a large proportion of most people's wealth is contained in the value of their homes.

(a) Who can claim

A claim for legal rights may be made by the surviving spouse, or by a person who had been living with the deceased for long enough to be regarded as married by cohabitation with habit and repute. As well as legitimate children, illegitimate children can also claim. Adopted children can claim legal rights from their adoptive parents' estates but not from their natural parents' estates. Step-children and foster children have no claim at all however long they have been brought up by the deceased as part of his family. If one of the children is already dead his legitimate or adopted children can claim in his place.

(b) How much is the claim worth

The surviving spouse's legal rights amount to one-third of the value of the moveable property left after debts and expenses have been deducted. This fraction is increased to one-half if there are no children or their legitimate or adopted descendants. The children's legal rights amount to one-third of the net moveable property, but this is increased to one-half if there is no surviving spouse. This is divided among all the children equally, but each child's share remains the same whether the others claim or not. Where a child had been given money by the deceased to set him up in business or to provide for him on marriage, this reduces the value of his claim.

The surviving spouse and any of the children may have renounced their legal rights while the deceased was still alive, perhaps in return for other gifts made to them. A person who renounces in this way is treated as not surviving the deceased, so that he cannot claim legal rights nor can his children claim in his place.

(c) Legacy or legal rights

A claimant for legal rights who benefits under the will must choose between the two. Only if he renounces his legacy can he claim legal rights. Where the will doesn't deal with all the property, a spouse or child may claim their rights out of any unwilled estate (see Chapter 3), and can also claim legal rights out of moveable property covered by the will, or accept any legacies left to them.

Before making a decision whether to take the legacy or claim legal rights the respective values should be ascertained. Of course there are other factors to take into account in coming to this decision. Many people avoid making claims to prevent ill-feeling within the family. In particular a widow may feel upset if the children claim legal rights. Legal advice from an independent source may be helpful in coming to a decision.

(d) How is a claim made

A person wishing to claim legal rights should contact the deceased's executor or the lawyer acting for him. Proof of the claimant's relationship may be required. A person claiming to be married to the deceased by cohabitation with habit and repute may be asked to obtain a declaration from the court to this effect, while an illegitimate child claiming legal rights may be required to produce a birth certificate naming the father, a decree of affiliation or evidence that his father had admitted paternity. There is no need to go to court to obtain legal rights unless the executor refuses to pay.

An example may perhaps make clear the way legal rights work.

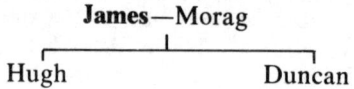

James—Morag

Hugh   Duncan

James dies leaving a house worth £15,000. The rest of his property (all moveable) e.g. furniture, car, money and investments amounts to £12,000. James had been separated from his wife Morag for some years before his death, and apart from leaving his elder son Hugh £3,000 and his other son Duncan £1,000, he leaves the rest of his property to his mistress. Morag decides to claim her legal rights. As there are also surviving children she receives £4,000 i.e. one-third of £12,000. If either son decided to claim legal rights his share would amount to £2,000 i.e. one-half of £4,000 (one-third of £12,000). Duncan may well decide to claim his legal rights as he will get more that way than if he accepts his legacy. On the other hand Hugh will be better off with his legacy of £3,000.

CHAPTER 5.

Distributing the Estate

This chapter is directed at the executors. It describes the rules and sequence in which the estate is distributed to the various claimants and beneficiaries, and explains why administering an estate takes so long.

Payment of debts

All the deceased's debts must be paid out of his estate (whether heritable or moveable) before anything can be distributed by the executor to beneficiaries. Debts include funeral and administrative expenses.

If, after investigating the deceased's financial position, the executor finds out that he died bankrupt he should not bother to obtain confirmation. The creditors should be informed and left to take such steps as they think advisable. Very occasionally an estate becomes insolvent after confirmation has been obtained. This happens when additional creditors come forward afterwards. As soon as it is apparent that the debts exceed the assets, the executor should seek legal advice and inform all the creditors that the estate is insolvent. The creditors usually then ask the court to appoint someone to administer the estate under the court's supervision.

Death bed and reasonable funeral expenses (not including the cost of any headstone) have priority over all other debts, whether secured, privileged or ordinary. These should be paid as soon as money is available.

Next come secured debts. A debt is secured when a creditor holds an item of property as security against non-payment. Examples are a building society loan for which the house is a security, an unpaid repair bill for which the garage retains the car as security, and an overdraft for which a bank is holding a life insurance policy as security. Executors must make arrangements for paying the secured creditor when they wish to sell or distribute the property over which the security exists. Even where there is not enough money to pay privileged or ordinary debts, the secured debts must be paid. A building society may be willing to continue the existing loan if the beneficiary who is to take over the house can keep up the instalments. New legal documents will be necessary to give effect to this arrangement. If a house with a loan over it is bequeathed, the loan is repayable by the beneficiary. It is not a debt payable from the estate unless the will says otherwise.

After secured debts come privileged debts. The most common examples are the cost of obtaining confirmation and up to one year's arrears of rates and taxes. If the deceased was in business and owed wages to any employees, these are privileged up to a maximum of £800 per employee. Executors can pay these debts when they have money to do so without risk of challenge by later ordinary creditors. For arrears of taxes the precise amount due may not be known for some while. The likely amount due, including interest if chargeable, should be set aside to meet this liability.

Those debts (apart from funeral and death bed expenses) which are neither secured nor privileged are called ordinary debts. All ordinary creditors are entitled to be treated equally (i.e. to be paid the whole of their debts or, if there is not enough money, the same proportion) provided they take legal action to enforce payment within six months of death. Strictly, executors should not pay any legacies or ordinary debts until this period has elapsed. If they do, they run the risk that after paying all the known creditors, another creditor will come along within the six month period, and there will be insufficient money left to pay him in full. Executors who find themselves in this position may have to recover property already distributed, or even to pay the later creditor out of their own pockets.

Creditors who claim after the six month period are of course still entitled to payment of their debts. If all the money has been distributed, the creditors must recover their debts from the beneficiaries. These may have to refund all or part of their legacies, unless the creditor has delayed unreasonably in making his claim.

It is a bit hard on ordinary creditors to have to wait six months for settlement of their accounts. Executors should use their common sense here. If there is plenty of money and the deceased was clearly not bankrupt, it is probably safe to pay all the debts as soon as there is money available to meet them.

Legal rights

After paying the deceased's debts the next step, where a will is left, is to find out whether anyone is going to claim legal rights (see page 38). It can be very embarrassing if someone claims legal rights after most of the property has been distributed. Each of the possible claimants (usually the surviving spouse and any children) should be written to with a note of the value of their legal rights, and the suggestion that they take legal advice. Failure to decide whether to claim within two years of the death can lead to extra capital transfer tax being payable.

Acceptance of legacies

The executor informs all beneficiaries of their legacies. This provides an opportunity for any person who does not wish to accept his legacy to say so, but a decision to renounce should not be taken without careful thought. Non-acceptance of a legacy of money or of a particular item will increase the value of the residue of the estate, while non-acceptance of the legacy of the residue will mean the residue becomes unwilled.

It is possible for beneficiaries to get together and decide to redistribute the property in a completely different way from that laid down by the deceased in his will. This used to be uncommon, but since the introduction of capital transfer tax, such rearrangements occur more often. Large amounts of capital transfer tax may sometimes be saved by a redistribution.

Distribution of the Estate

After all the debts have been paid, the deceased's property is distributed according to the will or in terms of the legal rules which apply where there is no will. This is the most important part of dealing with an estate and it should be done very carefully. Any mistake may be difficult to put right and at the very least may lead to a lot of bad feeling. In some cases executors (or their lawyers) may have to recompense those who have lost out of their own pockets if the errors were due to negligence.

A complete list should be drawn up of what property there is, and to whom it is to go. Where there is a will it should be looked at again very carefully. If there is some doubt about its meaning, instead of going to court, the beneficiaries may agree on the interpretation to be adopted or may reach some compromise. Unless the will gives a specific item (e.g. a car) all a beneficiary is strictly entitled to is money, not any of the property that belonged to the deceased. Problems may arise if furniture or things that cannot be easily divided are left to more than one person. If no decision can be reached on who is to have what, the executor's duty is to sell and divide out the money received. This threat is usually enough to make people come to some sort of agreement. Sometimes somebody would like to take an item which is worth more than their entitlement. For example one of the children might wish the house. One solution to this problem is for the item to be taken at the value placed on it in the inventory (see page 9) or at a new valuation and for the extra to be paid into the estate by the person taking the item.

First, the named items should be made over to the beneficiaries. For items such as furniture, jewellery or a car the people concerned should be contacted and told that the items are now available for them to collect. If there is clearly more property than debts, the small items at least can be safely distributed as soon as confirmation has been obtained if not before. People must be prevented from helping themselves as it is all too easy for this sort of behaviour to get out of control.

The next task is probably to pay the legacies of money. It is a good idea to try and pay all such legacies at the same time. In periods of inflation even a few months' delay can mean an appreciable diminution in the value of the legacy. Interest may be claimable on a legacy if there has been unreasonable delay in paying it and if the executor has been obtaining interest himself on the estate under his control. Paying all the legacies together avoids any grumbles about one beneficiary being favoured over another. If the legacy is large then one or more payments to account could be made rather than delay the whole payment until enough money is to hand to pay it in full.

Premium Bonds cannot be transferred to a beneficiary even if he has been left them under the will. They can be held for up to a year after death by the executor, but after this they should be encashed, as they are no longer eligible for prizes.

National Savings Certificates and British Savings Bonds can be transferred by means of special application forms obtainable from main Post Offices. Shares are transferred by means of stock transfer forms for each holding. These forms are signed by the executor, stamped by the Inland Revenue and sent to the companies concerned. In a short while new certificates in the names of the beneficiaries will be returned. Division can present problems. If the individual investments are large in value then it is worthwhile splitting them, but for everyone to end up with a few shares of this and that is pointless. It is better to sell small holdings and distribute the cash instead. The beneficiaries should be asked whether they agree to any particular way of dealing with the shares. It is often helpful to get a stockbroker's advice first so that his recommendations can be passed on.

The sale or transfer of the house is a job for a lawyer, as the documents have to be prepared strictly in accordance with legal requirements. The executor should be consulted over the details of the transfer (e.g. price, entry date, what is included in the sale) but can leave the mechanics to the lawyer.

Receipts or acknowledgements for any payments made or items made over should always be obtained. Unless this is done it may be impossible to prove that beneficiaries have received all the money or property to which they were entitled, or that money said by the executor to have been spent by him on expenses, such as removals, really were paid for this purpose.

The final stages

Before the estate can be wound up all taxes due must be paid. First, the income tax position should be settled with the Inland Revenue. Then, if the estate is large enough for capital transfer tax to be payable this must be finalised as well. When this has been done, the Capital Taxes Office will on request issue a certificate which states that no further tax is due on the basis of the information submitted to them. This certificate does not prevent further tax being claimed if additional property comes to light afterwards, or if there has been evasion or fraud.

When the debts, taxes and legacies of money or property have been dealt with, an account of the estate should be drawn up. This account is a balance sheet. On one side is shown what property was taken over from the deceased, together with any interest, dividends or other payments received since death. The other side shows the debts, taxes, expenses and legacies paid and any money or property still in hand. The purpose of the account is to be able to show where all the property has gone to. It is surprising how often drafting the account brings some forgotten item or debt to light. If there is still money in hand the oversight can be put right, without having to ask for money back from beneficiaries. For this reason the account should be drafted before the estate is distributed completely. When all the problems have been sorted out, final payments can be made to any beneficiaries who had not received their full entitlement.

Where a lawyer is handling the estate, he will prepare the account and send it to the executor for approval. It is usual to send a copy to any residuary beneficiary as well so that he can see how the value of his legacy of residue has been calculated. Where interest or dividends have been received during the course of administration, a certificate showing the amount received and tax deducted should be sent to the residuary beneficiary, to enable him to include these payments in his own income tax return.

The executor's job is finished when all the property has been distributed and all the debts and taxes paid. There is no need in law to get a formal discharge from the beneficiaries. It is however a good idea for the lawyer at least to get the executor to sign the final account as approved and for some evidence of the residuary beneficiaries' approval to be kept as well. The signed copy of the final account or other evidence of approval should be kept in case disputes arise later. All the various papers, receipts and statements should be kept for a reasonable length of time until it is clear that no further problems or queries are going to arise. Then all except the will, the confirmation and the final account could be thrown out. These documents should be retained as they can often be needed several years later. If a trust has been set up by the will all the papers should be kept until the trust comes to an end.

Why it takes so long

One of the most frequent questions asked about distributing a person's property after he dies is why it takes so long. People often fail to understand why they can't have their money immediately after a death, and if a lawyer is involved they suspect him of inactivity or worse. A very simple estate can be disposed of within a month or two, but a complex one may take years without anybody really dragging their feet. The reasons for the delay are many and not all of them will be applicable in every case. Executors can help prevent complaints about delay by keeping beneficiaries in the picture and by distributing any money that they have as quickly as possible. They should make payments to account instead of waiting for a long time to pay in full.

First, there are a lot of steps to go through — investigating the property, obtaining confirmation, collecting in and selling the property and, finally, distributing it. All of these steps, which have to be done one after the other, involve writing letters, waiting for answers, and dealing with offices and organisations, who may not be able to give immediate attention to the documents submitted. Beneficiaries may have to be consulted and given time to think about what they wish done with various articles. Many forms have to be sent to executors for signature. This can take a long time especially if there are more than two executors or an executor is abroad.

Second, debts must be paid first, and executors should strictly wait for at least six months before paying creditors, let alone anyone else. With an estate that clearly has more property and money than likely debts there is not much risk involved in paying the known creditors and distributing most, if not all of the property before the six months are up. An executor is not obliged to take such a risk, and this should be explained to people who press for early payment.

A third reason is that the position regarding income tax and capital transfer tax can take a long time to sort out. Property may need to be valued and the value negotiated. If the deceased was self-employed the accounts of his business have to be prepared and agreed with the Inland Revenue. Even in simple cases where these sorts of problems don't occur it may take a few months to finalise the income tax position. The Inland Revenue cannot be expected to drop all the other cases they are dealing with in order to concentrate on one particular estate.

Finally, most lawyers are busy people who do various jobs for very many clients. Some work, like criminal trials, civil actions and buying and selling houses, involve deadlines which must be met. It is only sensible for the lawyer to make sure that this type of work receives priority. This means that the work connected with distributing a person's property may have to be fitted in when time is available. A courteous enquiry from the executor or a beneficiary as to the reason for delay will often work wonders, as the file is then promoted to the top of the pile. If this and further enquiries fail to produce a satisfactory response, then a formal complaint to the Law Society of Scotland may have to be considered.

CHAPTER 6.

Making a Will

This chapter is directed at all readers, seeking to convince them of the value of making a will. It discusses the question of whether to write a will oneself or instruct a lawyer, what form a will should take, what are the typical provisions in a will, how to ensure that it is a valid will, and how and when to alter or cancel a will. Documents other than wills making provision for others to inherit the deceased's property or money are also discussed. The chapter ends with a few practical hints and reminders for those wishing to write their own will, or at least to do the preparatory work for the lawyer.

What is a will?

A will is a document which sets out how a person wishes his or her property to be dealt with on death. Previously the word "testament" was used. This is occasionally met with in expressions such as "last will and testament", and a person making a will is still referred to in legal language as a testator. In addition to dealing with the disposal of property, a will normally appoints executors to carry out the deceased's intentions. It may also appoint tutors or curators (guardians) for children, contain directions for the funeral or gift the body or parts of it for medical purposes.

Wills are important, for unless a person leaves a will, his property is disposed of in a fixed manner according to legal rules (see Chapter 3). Nearly two-thirds of all people in Scotland die without having made a will. Some people put off making a will because it involves them in considering their own death. Others feel that they have little property worth dealing with and that wills are not for them. An additional barrier to making a will can be not knowing a lawyer to go to.

Why make a will?

There are five good reasons for making a will:

(1) You can decide how to leave your property. Money cannot be left to charities or friends outside the family without a will, nor can different amounts be given to each of the children. Even if the bulk of the money would go to the same people, whether a will was made or not, it is often nice to be able to leave small legacies to people or organisations you have known for a long time. The parcelling out of jewellery or small items, often of only sentimental value, may

cause more family feuding than much larger items and a will is a sensible way of avoiding this particular trouble.

(2) It saves the family worry. A death is a difficult enough time for the survivors without extra problems arising from the lack of a will and executors to look after any property.

(3) By making an appropriate will it may be possible to save capital transfer tax if the total property left (together with previous large gifts) exceeds £50,000.

(4) There may be extra legal costs in disposing of a person's property if there is no will. An executor may have to be appointed by the court and a guarantee found for his proper administration.

(5) A will can contain directions for the funeral, gift the body or parts of it for medical purposes and appoint tutors or curators (guardians) to look after children who might become orphans. Even if both parents are alive, they should consider the possibility of both dying at the same time, in a road accident for example.

Do you need a lawyer?

As a will is such an important document it is vital that it is correct otherwise it may be invalid (see page 33). The provisions must be clear and the whole document be in correct legal form. The easiest way to ensure this is to go to a lawyer and ask him to prepare the will. On the present scale of fees about £10-£15 would be charged for a short simple will, although more complex wills, which involve a lot of consultation and drafting, will cost considerably more. This expense is well worth while for the peace of mind in having a will which will stand up and be interpreted in accordance with your wishes. The lawyer's fee can be paid for under the legal advice and assistance scheme if the client has less than a certain amount of disposable capital and income (see Appendix VI).

Finding a lawyer can be a problem if the person wishing to make a will does not already know one. Appendix V contains guidance on how to get hold of a lawyer in these circumstances. Most lawyers will call to see clients who are too ill or handicapped to visit their offices, although an extra charge may be made for such a service to cover travelling time.

Even if a lawyer is to be instructed to prepare a will it is wise to spend time working out exactly what you have to leave and to whom you want it to go before you visit the lawyer.

Many people feel that they can make their own will without going to a lawyer. Some people write their own wills, others use printed will forms which can be bought in bookshops and stationers. Experience shows that all too often a home-made will is inaccurate, uncertain or wrongly signed and witnessed, so that disputes and litigation arise after death. The expense of sorting this out may far outweigh the modest fee a lawyer would have charged for making a proper will in the first place.

Who can make a will?

In general anyone can make a will unless they are completely insane or too young. Even insane people can make a will if done in a lucid interval. To prevent challenge after death, certificates should be obtained from doctors declaring that the person was lucid i.e. mentally fit to make a will and to understand what he was doing. Since 1964 girls above 12 and boys above 14 have been able to leave their whole property by will, provided they are domiciled in Scotland. Disabled people who are unable to write or illiterates can still make a will. The will can be prepared according to their wishes and signed on their behalf by a lawyer or minister (see page 52).

Form of a will

The only formalities that Scots law requires for a will are that it must be in writing and authenticated in one of the ways described on page 51. There is no need for special paper or seals. One woman wrote what was to happen to her property in a letter to her daughter. This was held to be a valid will, but it is not an example which ought to be followed.

No special form of words is required. All that the law demands is that the document taken as a whole shows that a will was intended, and that it is the final version not just a draft. Phrases such as "after my death" or "I bequeath to" or the appointment of executors are all strong pointers to a will rather than to lifetime gifts. The usual evidence of finality is the person's signature at the end. A person only signs any important document when he is quite sure it is what he wants. The three examples of wills in Appendix IV illustrate all these points. Although it is not essential, a will should say when it was signed. Where more than one will is left, it is easy to see which is the latest if both are dated.

Types of provisions found in wills

A will is a document which expresses the wishes of the deceased as to how his property is to be divided after death. There are various types of provisions a will can contain to give effect to his intentions, all of which have their uses in appropriate situations.

(a) Universal legacy

The simplest will merely leaves all the property to another person. Such a provision creates no problems in distribution or interpretation but, with the exception of spouses, not many people want to leave all their property to one particular member of the family, and to ignore the others.

(b) Ordinary legacy

Another type of legacy is a bequest of money or specific property. Examples are "I leave £200 to my son Alexander" or "I bequeath to my nephew, Ian Mackenzie, my golf clubs". These are both straightforward gifts; Alexander and Ian will receive their money and golf clubs respectively when the person making the will dies, provided there is money available and that the golf clubs have not been previously disposed of. This type of legacy can be used to give small remembrances to relatives and friends or to distribute substantial sums of money or items of property (e.g. a house) amongst the family.

(c) Residuary legacy

A bequest of residue disposes of the residue or remainder of a person's property after all the other legacies and provisions of the will have been implemented. All properly prepared wills contain a residue clause, since no one can know exactly what property he will have when he dies. Besides it is usually impossible for a person to list all the property he possesses and it is unwise to attempt to do so. If any item is missed out and there is no bequest of residue, the omitted item must be treated as unwilled. The value of a bequest of residue can vary enormously, depending on the size and value of the other bequests and the amount of property the deceased leaves.

(d) Trusts

A trust is set up when property is given to named persons (called trustees) to be held by them and used for particular purposes. The purposes must be legal and useful, otherwise the trust will be disregarded. The purposes of the trust must be set out plainly in the will because if it is not clear what the money is to be used for, the trust will be void. The courts will however supply any necessary administrative details that were omitted.

A very important use of trusts is to give someone a liferent. The property is given to trustees who have to allow that person (the liferenter) the use of it during his lifetime. On the death of the liferenter the trustees hand the property over to another person (the fiar) named by the deceased in his will. Where money or investments are liferented the liferenter only receives the interest or dividends but cannot touch the capital. A liferenter of a house is normally entitled to live there or let it but cannot sell it. Liferents are often used to provide for a widow(er) and yet make sure that the property eventually passes to the children. If a straightforward gift is made the surviving spouse can fritter away the inheritance or leave it to his or her own family. A drawback is that the liferenter may find it difficult to make ends meet on the annual income when the cost of living increases. He or she can be helped to some extent if the trustees are given power in the will to lend or give capital to the liferenter. Liferents can also be used to prevent spendthrift children squandering their inheritances, or to provide for children who are incapable of looking after themselves.

Trusts are also used when money is to be left to young children. A small bequest left to a child can be paid to the parents to spend or invest on his behalf. For substantial gifts a trust is preferable, and in this case the will should state what the trustees are to do with the income (e.g. pay for school fees or holidays) and when the capital is to be given to the child.

Trusts are used to provide annual prizes or bursaries for schools or universities out of the income from property given to the trustees. Where the deceased wishes to give money to carry out some scheme (e.g. build an opera house) trustees may have to be appointed to administer the scheme.

The expenses of administration usually make trusts not worth while unless large sums are involved.

Other provisions

Executor
Besides disposing of the deceased's property a will usually appoints an executor or executors to carry out the provisions of the will and administer the property after death. If the will fails to appoint an executor the court will do so (see page 6) but this involves extra expense and delay.

Disposal of body
A will may also contain directions for the funeral or disposal of the body after death. The deceased's next of kin have a veto over the body being disposed of in any way other than burial (see pages 2 and 3).

Care of children
Finally a will may appoint tutors or curators (guardians) to any children under 18 years of age. These people will act together with the surviving parent if any. Such a provision is usually only inserted in the will of a widow(er), as the surviving parent of a married couple automatically becomes the tutor or curator of any children. A wife or husband may wish, however, to appoint tutors or curators to guard against the possibility of both parents dying in the same accident.

Methods of authenticating a will

(a) Attested will
An attested will is signed by the person making the will and by two witnesses above fourteen years old. An example of an attested will is shown in Appendix IV No. 1. Each of the witnesses must see the person sign or hear him acknowledge his signature. They need not be present together, nor need they know what the document is about. The addresses of the witnesses must be given, either at the end of the will or below their signatures (see Appendix IV No. 2). If the will is on more than one sheet of paper, each page must be signed at the bottom by the person making the will. Failure to follow these requirements in any respect may make the will invalid. Although one spouse can witness the other's will and a person benefiting from a will can act as a witness, it is better to get independent witnesses if possible. If the will is challenged later, evidence from a spouse or a person benefiting will obviously be treated with caution. The great advantage of an attested will is that it is accepted as formally valid until it is successfully challenged. The challengers must convince the court that it is a forgery or that there was something wrong with the way it was signed

or witnessed. This is usually very difficult to do and for this reason a lawyer will always prepare an attested will for a client. A disadvantage is that two witnesses are necessary and these may not always be available. It is a good idea to go to a bank to get a home-made will witnessed. The staff are familiar with the legal requirements thus ensuring that the will is at least correctly signed and witnessed.

If the person making the will is unable to sign it, this can be done for him. A solicitor or the minister of the parish may sign on behalf of the person making the will, if he has, in the presence of two witnesses, read the will over to the person and asked for and received authority to sign. The solicitor or minister then signs, adding a statement as to what was done. The procedure and the statement must be in exact compliance with the law.

(b) Holograph

A holograph will is one written entirely in a person's own handwriting (see Appendix IV No. 3). It is valid provided it is signed at the end. No witnesses are necessary. A document may be treated as holograph although it is typed (or written by someone else) if above his signature the person writes *in his own handwriting* the words "adopted as holograph". This is a very useful device as it avoids having to write out the whole will. A holograph or "adopted as holograph" will is valid, but if challenged it is up to those saying it is valid to convince the court that this is so. This may be difficult because a person's writing can often change near death, and there are no witnesses to the will to give evidence. One advantage is that witnesses are not needed, so that a person can prepare his own will in secret. Even a visit to a lawyer to get a will made can be difficult to arrange without the whole family getting to know. Another advantage is that a holograph will only has to be signed at the end to make it valid, and most people will remember to do this.

(c) Will forms

A will form may be obtained from many booksellers or stationers. It consists of a large printed form with blanks, which the person making the will fills up to show his name and address, the bequests he is making, the executors he is appointing etc. When complete the document is meant to be signed in the presence of two witnesses, so making it an attested will (see page 51).

A will form is a cheap and easy way of making a home-made will. However, the person does have to be good at following the accompanying instructions (often based on *English* law) and filling up forms correctly. A danger is that if the signing and witnessing is not done correctly the will may be invalid. A will form should only be used to make a simple will as there is only limited space to write out the provisions.

(d) Other documents

A document which is not a will in itself can form part of a will. The will may provide that any future list of bequests that has been merely signed is to be effective. Many people change their minds frequently about which members of the family are to get particular items of jewellery or other personal possessions. Rather than put these legacies in the will, and then have to go to a lawyer every time a change is desired, lists of personal bequests can be drawn up and altered at home if the will authorises this. This type of list should not be used to make changes in the will. It should be dated so that if more than one exists it is easy to see which is the latest version.

Wills made outwith Scotland

Each country has its own requirements for executing i.e. signing and witnessing wills, but accepts a will made according to the law of another country, if the person making the will had some connection with that other country. A will is treated as validly executed if this was done according to:

(a) the law of the place where it was signed, or

(b) the law of the domicile (see glossary) of the maker of the will or of the territory in which he normally lived, or

(c) the law of a state of which he was a citizen.

In cases (b) and (c) the law can be either the law at the time of signing or the law at the date of death.

As an illustration of these rules a person living in Scotland who makes a will while on holiday in France can either execute it according to Scots law or French law. If he follows French law, then before it could be accepted in Scotland an expert in French law would have to certify that it was valid according to French law.

If the will was validly executed when it was signed then it remains valid, notwithstanding any future change in its maker's nationality, domicile or residence. A will made by a person when he lived in Scotland remains valid if he moves to England later. Similarly an English person need not make a new will just because he comes to live in Scotland.

Each country also has different legal rules about what must go in a will and the effect of various provisions in wills. Where a will was made outwith Scotland or made by a person who was not domiciled in Scotland, the legal rules which say whether foreign law or Scots law should be used to interpret it are very complex. Legal rights (see page 38) can be claimed out of the moveable property of any person who was domiciled in Scotland when he died, even if he was domiciled elsewhere when he made his will. A Scottish domiciled person who owns property (particularly a house or land) abroad should get advice from a lawyer there, as well as from a lawyer in Scotland, before making a will.

Other documents with testamentary effect

Other documents besides wills can dispose of property on a person's death. The ones most commonly met with in practice are nominations and survivorship destinations.

(a) Nominations

Many organisations allow a person to nominate to whom money or benefits due to him shall be paid on his death. National Savings Certificates, or money in the National Savings Bank, or with friendly or provident societies (such as life insurance and superannuation) can be nominated. A special form is obtained from the organisation, completed and returned to them. Apart from the National Savings Bank and National Savings Certificates, where there is no limit to the amount that may be nominated, there is a general limit of £1,500 per organisation. If all a person has is money in these sorts of organisations there may be no need to make a will at all. It is important not to forget a nomination and a copy should be kept as a reminder. The money cannot be left to someone else in a later will unless the nomination is first cancelled.

(b) Survivorship destinations

If the title to land or buildings is taken in the names of two people and then to the survivor of them, then on the death of one of them the property automatically passes to the other. A title like this is said to have a survivorship destination. It is common for a married couple to take the title to their house in this way. A survivorship destination should not be forgotten in making a will. What happens when a person makes conflicting provisions in a later will is described on page 36.

"Either and survivor" joint bank or building society accounts are different. On the first death the ownership of the balance may not pass to the survivor. Although the survivor can continue to draw money out of the account, he or she may have to hand it over to the person entitled to it, if the money was otherwise willed or is required for payment of debts or legal or prior rights (see Chapter 3).

Alteration of wills

In general the provisions of any will can be altered. A person's family circumstances and wishes change during his life and his will should reflect these changes. When children or grand-children are born or people marry, get divorced or die then a will should be altered. It is not a good idea, however, to change a will too frequently with every passing whim or fancy. Many elderly people are prone to do this and all too often they and their wills get confused and muddled. On the other hand, young people, once they have made their wills, tend to forget about them.

Once a will has been made the actual document should not be altered. Ineffective alterations are one of the commonest errors in home-made wills. Merely putting a line through a legacy or even initialling other alterations may not prevent the original provisions from remaining effective. If minor changes are desired the correct course is to prepare a codicil. This is a short document which refers to the original will and makes one or more alterations to it. An example is given in Appendix IV No. 2. The codicil should be attested (or signed if holograph) (see pages 51 and 52). If more than one or two changes are wished then it is better to cancel the first will and make a new one. There is less chance of confusion and error in setting out what is wanted in one document than in two documents which have to be read together. Similarly it is usually bad practice to have more than two codicils — it is better to start again with a new will.

When a will cannot be altered

A mutual will is one exception to the general rule that wills can always be altered. A mutual will is a *single* document in which *two* people leave their property to each other and, on the death of both, to others. For example, two sisters living together may each leave their property to each other and thereafter to their nephews and nieces. The surviving sister may be prohibited from altering the will and leaving the money to a charity instead of her nephews and nieces. Mutual wills should be avoided as their effect depends on the precise wording and circumstances. In the above example the same result could be better achieved by each sister leaving, in a separate will, her property in liferent (see page 50) to the other sister and thereafter to her nephews and nieces.

Cancellation of wills

A will can be revoked or cancelled by saying so in a later will. The phrase commonly used is "I revoke all previous testamentary writings". "Testamentary writings" is used rather than "wills" as it has a wider meaning. It would include a separate signed list of bequests that forms part of a will but is not a will in itself. On making a new will the previous will should be revoked, otherwise two valid wills will be left. If this happens the estate will probably be distributed in a completely different way from that intended by the deceased in his second will (see page 36).

Planning a will

Before you start writing out your will you should think about it carefully. Even if you are having a will prepared by a lawyer you must be able to tell him how you want your property disposed of. A rough idea will give him something to work on.

The first step is to list all your property with an approximate indication of its value. Remember to include insurance policies and any other sums which will be paid after your death. Deduct any debts and any building society loan. If you are worth over £100,000 a substantial proportion of your estate will be swallowed up in capital transfer tax. This tax is payable out of the residue of your property, so don't be too generous with other legacies. The person who is left a house must pay a proportion of any tax due; the amount depending on how much the house is worth compared to the total value of the estate.

Next think to whom you want to leave most of your property, starting with your immediate family. If you are married with children there are many ways in which you can divide your estate. When the children are young the whole estate could be left to your surviving spouse on the basis that he or she is going to have to look after them for some time. If you want to do this and have only a modest amount of money then it may be best not to leave any property by your will at all (but you might wish to say who is to take care of your children). If a will is left any children can claim legal rights (see page 38) even if you don't want them to get anything, but if there is no property left by the will then the surviving spouse is almost certain to inherit everything by virtue of prior rights (see page 23). Where you want to provide for your spouse as far as possible, and yet ensure that the property eventually passes to the children, then a trust giving your spouse a liferent (see page 50) may be the answer. this is generally only worth considering if you have quite a lot of money or own your own home, because even the simplest trust involves administrative costs.

Other possible arrangements in providing for your spouse and children are legacies to the children with the residue of the estate going to your spouse, or a legacy or legacies to your spouse (e.g. the house, furniture and some money) with the children getting the residue. Remember you can't disinherit your spouse and children completely as they can claim legal rights (see page 38). There can be capital transfer tax advantages if the first parent to die leaves something to the children by will. If you are leaving substantial legacies to young children, you may wish to set up trusts for them.

If you have no immediate family, perhaps you have other relations you wish to leave money to. Again trusts may be useful where young children are involved. Many people, however, prefer to leave their money to charities rather than to distant relatives.

Once you have settled the major provisions you can think about any small gifts you might like to make to friends or charities. Perhaps you wish to leave certain of your cherished possessions to particular people rather than have them all go to the person who inherits the furniture or the residue.

Once you have settled on a rough scheme it is useful to go through your list of property seeing who is to get what. Sometimes you find that you have forgotten some items. If you are leaving a house or land to somebody they will have to pay any capital transfer tax due on it. This can cause problems if you wish to leave a house to someone who is not otherwise well off. One solution is to provide in your will that the tax is to be payable out of the residue of your estate, rather than by the person receiving the house.

One of the most important decisions is the choice of executors. The Public Trustee service, under which state officials can act as executors for people in England and Wales, is not available in Scotland. You should choose people in whom you have confidence to carry out the provisions of your will properly and fairly. At least two executors should be chosen to guard against the possibility of one dying suddenly and leaving no one to continue. Select people younger than yourself since they are likely to outlive you. It is a good idea to have at least one member of the family as an executor and also someone who is reasonably familiar with business and financial matters. Being an executor can be a worrying and time-consuming task, even though a solicitor normally helps with the legal aspects. See if the people you have in mind are willing to act before you appoint them. Executors cannot claim any fee for their services unless you say so in your will, but the expense of employing a solicitor comes out of the estate. Often family executors may be left small legacies as a token of appreciation for their services.

Some people appoint banks as their executors. Banks have special departments to deal with wills and the staff there have ready access to all the investment and financial expertise in the bank's other departments. On the other hand there is a lack of personal touch that you can get from your own choice of executors aided by a family lawyer. Also banks are not very interested in dealing with small estates and they will usually charge more than a lawyer would. If you decide to use a bank as your executor then discuss the matter with your bank manager. He will get your will prepared, with the appropriate clauses, either by your own solicitor or by a firm that the bank uses for its own business.

Having disposed of your property and appointed executors, you may wish to give directions for your funeral (e.g. a desire to be cremated) or for gifting parts or all of your body for medical purposes. If you have young children you may wish to appoint tutors or curators (guardians) in case they are orphaned on your death.

Points to remember

1. Have you made any nomination? Have you a share of a house or land which is held under a survivorship destination? If so does your will take these into account (see page 54)?

2. Have you got the correct names and addresses of all the people you are leaving something to? Are all your gifts clearly and unambiguously described? If you own your house and leave it to somebody, remember you might be living somewhere else when you die. Provide for this by saying "my house at 25 Richard Place, Edinburgh, or such other house as I may own at the time of my death."

3. Have you disposed of the residue or remainder of your estate (see page 50)?

4. Have you considered that the people you are leaving legacies to might die before you? Have you made alternative provisions at least for the residue?

5. Have you appointed executors (see page 6)?

6. If you already have a will have you cancelled it (see page 55)?

The language of a will

If you are writing your own will try to express yourself as clearly and simply as possible. Avoid legal phrases as they may have a meaning quite the opposite to what you thought they had. Some of the commonest words can lead to the most difficult problems in the interpretation of wills.

"I leave . . . to my children"

An adopted child would not share in any bequest to children in a will made before 10 September 1964 unless he was specifically mentioned but where the will was made after that date adopted children are included. A child that is jointly adopted by a couple is treated as their legitimate child for every family relationship.

An illegitimate child would not share in any bequest to children in a will made before 25 November 1968 unless the will very clearly said so, but in wills made since then an illegitimate child is included.

Children born after the date of the will are included. A child *in utero* (i.e. conceived but not yet born) at the date of death of the deceased will be entitled to share in a legacy to children, provided it is born alive.

Stepchildren have no blood relationship to the deceased and are not treated as his children even if they were brought up by him as members of his family. If a step-child is to be left a legacy he must be specially mentioned apart from the deceased's children. A step-child cannot claim legal rights either (see page 39), "Children" do not include grandchildren or remoter descendants.

"I leave . . . to my wife"

A divorce after the date of the will will not result automatically in a wife losing her legacy, especially if she has been described by name as well (e.g. my wife, Mrs Margaret Inglis or Macpherson). Where the deceased divorced and remarried after making his will, there is no fixed rule favouring either the former wife or the second wife. Which person receives the legacy depends on whether the will as a whole indicates that the gift is to an individual or is to a wife as part of a family settlement. However, if the former wife is described by name, the second wife can never benefit under the will, although she may claim legal rights (see page 38).

(c) "When he comes of age"

In setting up trusts for children it is common to state an age when they will receive the capital set aside for them. A popular choice is 21 for if the child has not acquired financial sense by then, he or she is unlikely ever to do so. Instead of stating the age in years, phrases such as "age of majority" or "when he comes of age" are often used. In wills made before the Age of Majority Act 1969 this means 21, but in wills made since then it means 18.

"I leave my money to . . ."

"Money" should never be used in a will because it has no definite meaning. How a legacy of money will be interpreted by the courts depends on the other provisions of the will. It may include investments, furniture or even a house, as well as cash, and the meaning given may be quite contrary to what was intended by the deceased.

Correct description

It is important when making a will to describe what is given and to whom it is given as fully and clearly as possible. People should be given their full names and addresses and not just described as "my nephew". That description might have been sufficient when the person making the will had only one nephew, but it makes for confusion if another nephew is born afterwards. Objects should be described accurately enough to distinguish them from any other similar items. Don't just put "my brooch" say "my silver leaf brooch". Check the correct names of any charities or organisations to which money is being left. To leave money to the "Royal Society for Prevention of Cruelty to Children" is ambiguous for either the "Royal Scottish Society for Prevention of Cruelty to Children" or the "National Society for Prevention of Cruelty to Children" might have been intended. These misdescriptions or ambiguous descriptions are only resolvable by looking at other evidence. For example if the deceased had been involved with the Royal Scottish Society, but never with the National Society then it is much more likely the former was intended. If after all the evidence has been considered it is still not clear whom or what was meant, then the bequest is invalid.

Writing out a will

Once you have decided what to put in the will do several drafts until you are satisfied that you know exactly what you are going to write. Don't write in pencil: use a pen or biro or better still type. If you make a mistake don't rub anything out or attempt to alter it — start again. Finally, remember to sign every page of the will and have it witnessed correctly (see page 51), unless you are making a holograph will, in which case you only need sign at the end and no witnesses are required.

Glossary of Legal Terms

beneficiary — a person who inherits property from the deceased or who benefits from a trust.

bequeath — leave something (a bequest) by will

caution — a bond of caution is an undertaking to pay for any loss caused by a person's acts or default. Pronounced "kayshun".

codicil — a document making alterations to an existing will.

domicile — the place where the law considers a person's permanent residence to be or the place with which he has most connections.

confirmation — authority granted by a court in Scotland to an executor to administer the deceased's estate.

eik — a supplementary confirmation which must be obtained when additional estate is discovered after confirmation has been obtained. Pronounced "eek".

estate — all the property left by the deceased.

executor — a person who administers the estate of the deceased. An executor-nominate is an executor who has been nominated by the deceased in his will or who has been appointed by an executor-nominate. An executor-dative is one appointed by the court.

fiar — the person to whom liferented property passes on the death of the liferenter.

general legacy — a legacy of something which is not distinguished from other articles of the same kind which belonged to the deceased. The only common example is a legacy of money.

heritable — heritable property is land or buildings and nearly every interest (including a lease) in them.

holograph — a document entirely in one person's handwriting.

intestate — intestate estate is property not dealt with by any will or other document which transfers property on death. An intestate is a person who dies without leaving a valid will.

inventory — in the context of this book, a list of the deceased's heritable and moveable estate situated in the United

Kingdom together with any foreign moveable estate. The inventory does not include property passing under a survivorship destination or property which the deceased liferented. Loosely, the Inland Revenue forms are referred to as inventories.

issue — legitimate or adopted descendants.

legal rights — the rights of a surviving spouse and/or descendants to a share of the deceased's moveable estate.

legatee — a person who is left a legacy.

liferent — the use and enjoyment of property only for the duration of a person's (the liferenter's) lifetime.

litigation — court proceedings to make a claim or settle a dispute.

moveable — moveable property is articles capable of being moved, most rights and paper assets like life policies, shares and debts. A debt which is secured over land is part of the creditor's heritable property.

nomination — a method of leaving money held by or due from certain organisations (see page 54) otherwise than by will.

petition — a document in which the court is asked to authorise some act.

plenishings — domestic articles in a house other than personal possessions. A car is not usually regarded as a plenishing.

prior rights — the rights available to a surviving spouse when the deceased died without a will.

privileged debt — a debt which is given priority when there is insufficient money left to pay all the deceased's debts in full (see page 41).

procurator fiscal — the official responsible for investigating suspected crimes and for prosecuting offenders in the sheriff and district courts.

reduction — the setting aside or annulment of a document by a court.

residue — the remainder of the estate after all the debts, taxes, expenses and other legacies have been met.

residuary beneficiary — a person who is left the residue or a share of residue.

revoke — cancel or render ineffective. A revocation clause in a will cancels all previous wills.

special legacy — a legacy of a particular item or group of items.

succession — the inheritance or transfer of property on death.

survivorship		
destination	— a destination in a title to land which, on the first death, transfers the property to the survivor of the original owners.	
testament	— see will.	
trust	— the gift or transfer of property to a person (the trustee) to hold or use it, not for his own benefit, but for the benefit of another (the beneficiary).	
will	— a document which sets out how a person wishes his estate to be disposed of on his death.	
void	— invalid and of no effect.	

APPENDIX II

Specimen Inventory

Estate in Scotland

1. House and garden at 10 Grange Gardens	£30,000		
Less sum due to Forth Building Society	10,000		
		£20,000	
2. Cash in house		27	
3. Furniture, plenishings and personal effects belonging to deceased at 10 Grange Gardens		7,500	
4. Cortina motor car registration number MPG 754D		200	
5. Arrears of salary (net) from Lothian Regional Council		287	
6. Royal Bank of Scotland Limited, 36 St Andrew Square, Edinburgh			
Sum at credit of current account No 213508		169	
7. Trustee Savings Bank, 28 Hanover Street, Edinburgh			
Sum at credit of account No 15724	153.75		
with interest (net) accrued	21.25		
		175	
8. Standard Life Limited, 3 George Street, Edinburgh Life Insurance Policy No C534712		10,500	
9. £2,000 9% Treasury Stock 1992-96 at 84		1,680	
10. Income Tax rebate say		1	
		£40,539	

Estate in England and Wales

11. Rose Cottage, Llangranog, Wales	8,000
12. British Petroleum Limited 400 Ordinary 25p shares at £3.50	1,400
13. Imperial Chemical Industries Limited 750 Ordinary Shares at £2	1,500
	£51,439

Summary for Confirmation

Estate in Scotland	£40,539
Estate in England and Wales	10,900
	£51,439

Moveable Estate elsewhere

Rank Xerox Inc. U.S.A. $200 Common Stock at $20 = $4,000 Converted to sterling at date of death	£1,956

Schedule of Debts

Funeral expenses	£257
Sum due to Lothian Regional Council being arrears of rates for 10 Grange Gardens, Edinburgh	143
Sum due to A. McDonald & Sons, 14 West Brighton Place, Edinburgh, for painter work at 10 Grange Gardens	85
	£485

APPENDIX III

Examples of the Distribution of Intestate Estates

Example I

A student Robert is killed while out climbing one weekend. His books and clothes are worth £200. He has £500 in the bank from his holiday job and grant and his old car is sold for £50 which just covers his debts. Robert is survived by his mother and two younger sisters Margaret and Lilias.

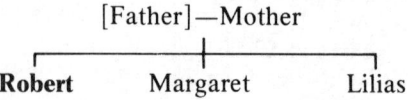

[Father]—Mother

Robert   Margaret   Lilias

Robert has no surviving spouse and no descendants, so there are no prior rights or legal rights. The net estate is worth £700 and is divided among the sisters and the mother as follows (the father having died before Robert):

Mother	£350
Margaret	£175
Lilias	£175

Example II

Jean dies of cancer in early middle age. She is survived by her husband John and two children Elizabeth and Peter. She owned the family house worth £20,000 and the furniture, plenishings etc. of no great value. In addition to her car valued at £2,000 and jewellery valued at £750, she had £1,250 in her bank account and £7,000 in investments.

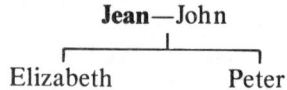

Jean—John

Elizabeth   Peter

John's prior rights are:

    (1) The house since it is worth less than £30,000.
    (2) The furniture and plenishings since they are below £8,000 in value.
    (3) £8,000 in cash as there are surviving children.

The rest of Jean's estate comes to £3,000 i.e. £11,000 minus £8,000 and is all moveable. John's legal rights are one-third of this sum (as there are children) i.e. £1,000.

The children's legal rights are also £1,000, which they share equally between them i.e. £500 each.

After prior and legal rights have been deducted the remainder of the estate amounts to £1,000. This is inherited by the children equally between them i.e. another £500 each. The final position is as follows:

John	House, plenishings and £9,000
Elizabeth	£1,000
Peter	£1,000

Example III

James' will leaves his wife Susan the house (but no mention is made of the furniture and plenishings) and his money in a particular building society account. His son Andrew was just left his golf clubs, as Andrew was doing well for himself, and James knew that Susan would leave everything to Andrew anyway when she died. There was no residue clause in the will. Just before he died James had withdrawn £8,000 from the building society account (leaving another £1,500 still there) and placed this sum in his bank, as he had intended to buy a new car.

Property covered by will   House, £1,500 in the building society account, golf clubs.

Unwilled property   Furniture and plenishings, £8,000.

James — Susan
|
Andrew

Although Andrew would be better off financially if he renounced his legacy of the golf clubs and claimed his legal rights, he decides not to claim. Susan takes the furniture and plenishings under her prior rights. She would also be entitled to £8,000 in cash as there are surviving children, but she must deduct the legacy of £1,500 which she receives. Her claim under prior rights is thus reduced to £6,500. After Susan's prior rights £1,500 is left for further division. This is money which is not covered by the will. Her legal rights amount to another third of this i.e. £500 and this is also the amount of Andrew's legal rights as well. The remainder of the estate amounts to £500, which goes to Andrew as the surviving child. Andrew does not have to give up his legacy of the golf clubs in order to receive this money, as it comes from money that is not dealt with by the will.

The final division is:

Susan: house (by will), furniture and plenishings (by prior rights), and £8,500 in cash (£1,500 by will, £6,500 by prior rights and £500 by legal rights).

Andrew: golf clubs (by will) and £1,000 (£500 legal rights and £500 remainder of the estate).

Styles of Wills

The styles of wills shown here are not as full as those prepared by lawyers. They are intended to show what form wills take and to illustrate some of the points made in the text.

1. Attested will

I, Ian Macdonald of 53 Marchmont Avenue, Edinburgh, make the following provisions regarding the distribution of my whole estate on my death:

(1) I leave my sister Miss Morag Macdonald of 17 Hillview, Edinburgh five hundred pounds (£500).

(2) I leave my brother Alexander Macdonald of 4 Dee Terrace, Aberdeen, my golf clubs, golf bag and trolley.

(3) I leave my son Hugh Macdonald, residing with me, my gold watch which belonged to my father.

(4) I leave the residue of my estate to my wife Mrs Janet Dalziel or Macdonald, residing with me.

I appoint my wife Janet and my son Hugh to be my executors, and I revoke all previous wills and testamentary writings: IN WITNESS WHEREOF I have signed this will at Edinburgh on 15 May 1979 before these witnesses James Mowat of 54 Marchmont Avenue, Edinburgh, and Hugh Sinclair of 17 Bruntsfield Hill, Edinburgh.

J Mowat witness Ian Macdonald

Hugh Sinclair witness

CODICIL

2. Attested codicil

I, Ian Macdonald of 53 Marchmont Avenue, Edinburgh, hereby alter my will dated 15 May 1979 in the following manner:

(a) The sum left to my sister Morag is to be increased from £500 to £1,000.

(b) I also leave the sum of £100 to the Royal National Institure for the Blind, 224 Great Portland Street, London.

IN WITNESS WHEREOF this codicil is signed by me at Edinburgh on 6 December 1979 before the following witness:

David Bruce, witness   *Ian Macdonald*

12 Nile Road, Glasgow.

Robt Taylor witness

47 West Claremont Street Edinburgh

3. Holograph will

45 Hamilton Drive
Stirling
1 December 1979

I leave all my property on my death to my wife Margaret or if she dies before me to my children equally.

Francis Gray.

Going to a Solicitor

How to find a solicitor

Most solicitors in Scotland handle problems relating to wills and estates. You may already have a "family lawyer" whom you could consult when making a will or in dealing with problems relating to settling the affairs of a friend or relative who has died. If you do not have a family lawyer, your friends may be able to recommend one.

A solicitor can usually be found by looking for a displayed Legal Aid sign on his office, or by consulting "Solicitors" in the yellow pages. However, more accurate information on the choice of solicitor available can be obtained by consulting either the local Legal Aid Secretary (under "Legal Aid" in the telephone directory) or a Citizens Advice Bureau, both of whom carry information on what types of work local solicitors are prepared to undertake and whether they handle legal aid work or not. The local library may also hold copies of the Legal Aid Solicitors Referral List or Law Society of Scotland's Directory of General Services. These provide information on lawyers and what types of work they are prepared to handle.

Making contact

It is advisable to call or telephone the solicitor's office beforehand and ask for an appointment to see him or her, explaining that it is a matter relating to making a will, being an executor under a will or claiming an inheritance, as appropriate. All relevant papers should be taken to the first meeting with the solicitor himself.

Paying for the solicitor

Most people go to a solicitor, obtain advice or instruct him to act on their behalf and in due course receive a bill for these services. In these cases it is advisable to enquire about costs at an early stage. Do not hesitate to ask the solicitor at the first interview roughly how much his services are likely to cost and how long the work is likely to take. If the case is complicated, you may need to discuss these questions again at a later interview. If at any stage you want a clearer idea how the work being done by the solicitor is progressing and what it is likely to cost, follow up verbal questions with a letter to the solicitor (keeping a copy).

Lower income clients may qualify for help under the Legal Advice and Assistance Scheme (see page 69). Even if your income means that you are unlikely to receive such assistance, it is possible to obtain at least initial advice at little or no cost. Many solicitors are prepared to give an initial interview of up to half an hour for no charge or up to not more than £5 inclusive of VAT. Solicitors subscribing to this Fixed Fee Interview Scheme are listed in the Legal Aid Solicitors Referral List, held by Legal Aid Secretaries, in the Directory of General Services and Citizens Advice Bureaux.

Members of the public may also seek preliminary information and advice from Citizens Advice Bureaux. Answers may be given by the bureau's own staff, or they may ask you to come back and see a lawyer, free of charge, at one of their legal clinics. If the case requires professional expertise, you will be advised to go to a lawyer's office, and the Citizens Advice Bureau may make an appointment for you to see a local solicitor.

APPENDIX VI

Legal Aid

Legal aid is money paid by the State to enable people who cannot afford lawyers to obtain legal help. There are two different schemes for non-criminal matters and both are administered by the Law Society of Scotland through their local legal aid committees. Most lawyers undertake legal aid work. A list of those that do can be obtained from the local Legal Aid Committee, a Citizens' Advice Bureau, or the clerk of the Sheriff Court.

Legal Advice and Assistance

Under this scheme a person may have up to £25 worth of legal help provided, although up to £50 will normally be authorised if an application is made for the increase. Almost any kind of work may be done, such as preparing a will, advising on and claiming legal rights and advising on the right to take over a tenancy. It is also useful for getting preliminary advice and evidence to see whether a legal aid application for litigation would be justified. Court and tribunal appearances are not covered but the lawyer may assist in preparing a case.

The scheme is free if the applicant's savings (excluding his house) are less than £600 (or a higher figure if he has dependants) and his net income (i.e. after tax, N.I. contributions and allowances for dependants) is below £40 per week. If his net income exceeds £85 per week or his savings exceed the above sum, no financial assistance can be given under this scheme. In between these limits the applicant pays a contribution assessed on a sliding scale. The limits change constantly and should be checked from time to time.

Legal Aid for civil proceedings

This scheme is designed to help people pursue or defend any civil action except defamation or breach of promise. It does not cover non-contentious matters such as house purchase or sale, or winding up a dead person's estate. Examples where legal aid may be available include litigation claiming legal rights, challenging a will or disputing its provisions.

In order to get legal aid the appropriate legal aid committee must be satisfied that a reasonable case exists. Preliminary advice and investigation may be needed to establish this. The legal advice and assistance scheme can be used for this work as legal aid generally only covers necessary court fees and expenses incurred after legal aid has been granted.

Even if a reasonable case exists legal aid will only be granted if the applicant's net income and capital are below certain limits. The income and capital of the applicant's spouse are also counted in unless the applicant is proceeding against his or her spouse. The financial part of the application is passed to the Department of Health and Social Security who assess what contributions are payable by the applicant. At present a man with a wife and two children would need to have less than £170 per week gross to qualify, while if he had less than £100 per week gross any legal aid would be completely free. In between these figures contributions are payable based on a sliding scale. The upper disposable capital limit over which legal aid will be refused is £2,500 while the lower limit below which no contribution is required is £1,200. Not all the value of a house is treated as capital.

A successful litigant normally has his expenses paid by his opponents. Where the legal aid committee recover these expenses in full from the opponents the legally aided person will have his contribution refunded. A refund may however take a long time to be paid.

A person who loses his case usually has to pay his opponents' expenses as well as his own. When the loser is legally aided the court normally modifies the total expenses payable by him to a sum it feels he can afford, but even so payments on top of the contribution already paid may be demanded. In some cases connected with wills or the distribution of estates the court may order the whole legal expenses of the proceedings to be paid out of the estate. Litigation is expensive and the expenses of going to court may swallow up a large part of the disputed estate or result in even a legally aided litigant being faced with a considerable bill for expenses. Every other way of settling a dispute should be tried before resorting to the courts.